Confessions of a Wayward Catholic

Confessions of a Wayward Catholic

FRANK SCOBLETE

Previously Published by
FSE PUBLISHING

authorHOUSE®

AuthorHouse™ LLC
1663 Liberty Drive
Bloomington, IN 47403
www.authorhouse.com
Phone: 1-800-839-8640

Previously Published by
FSE Publishing
PO Box 446
Malverme, NY 11565

1800-944-0406

Published by AuthorHouse   11/20/2013

ISBN: 978-1-4918-2426-9 (sc)
ISBN: 978-1-4918-2427-6 (hc)
ISBN: 978-1-4918-2428-3 (e)

Library of Congress Control Number: 2013918079

Contents

Sister Patricia Michael of the Sisters of Charity
Brother Jonathan of the Franciscan Brothers
Brother Barnabas of the Franciscan Brothers

You three made it all possible!

1

Mary Louise Roncallo

Bless me father for I have sinned.
I showed disgust for a fellow human being.

My first day of school at five years old. I wasn't nervous. I also wasn't all that interested. A lot of things my parents got excited about had no impact on me although if it were supposed to have a big impact on me I could pretend it did. The act of pretending I had learned so far back I couldn't remember when. I was what I pretended. The memory of a five-year old is as cloudy as the memory of anyone. As a five-year old, being four years old was 20 percent of my life ago. Hard to remember all of that.

"Now Frankie," said my mother, "I know you are nervous but kindergarten is your first step into the world of adulthood. Everything will be just fine."

"Yes," I said

We were living on 3rd Avenue and 70th Street (called Ovington Avenue) because my parents couldn't take the dirty fruit-man in the store below our old apartment on 62nd Street and 4th Avenue anymore. I didn't like that old apartment anyway because two rooms were not heated in the winter. My parents called it a "cold water flat."

I would be going to the local Catholic school, Our Lady of Angels on 74th Street between 3rd and 4th avenues. My mother dressed me in the standard Catholic blue knickers and a white shirt which had OLA lettered on it.

"Are you ready Frankie?" asked my father.

"Yes," I said.

Both my father and mother walked me the four blocks to the school. They held tightly to my hands, one on either side of me. The kindergarten was in its own small area of the grammar school. I guess they didn't want the older kids to torture the younger kids so they kept us separated.

The teacher, the ancient Sister Thomas Mahoney, who was maybe 40, stood outside the school and greeted all the parents and the new kindergartners. She seemed pleasant enough, although she looked a little fierce in her black and white habit which the nuns used to wear in those days.

Some of the kids cried and clung to their mothers—it was almost all mothers there, very few fathers. Some of the kids looked shell-shocked. Others, such as me, were just curious as to what this new chapter in our lives would entail.

"Sister! Sister!" yelled the skinny mother, smoke coming out of her nostrils. Mom seemed really agitated now. Sister Thomas came over. "My daughter is very nervous," said the skinny mother.

"Oh, she needn't be," said the nun in a kindly fashion to the skinny smoking mother and to the bloated girl. "My daughter has a delicate stomach," insisted the upset mother, smoke oozing out of her nose. "She gets very upset very easily." She inhaled deeply on her unfiltered cigarette. "She gets stomach aches."

"We'll take good care of her," said Sister Thomas. "What's your name?" Sister Thomas asked the girl. The girl buried her head in her mother's dress and made some weird choking sounds, "aaahhhh, urggghhh, dolpop."

"Her name is Mary Louise Roncallo," said the skinny woman, throwing her cigarette onto the ground. "Do you think I could stay in the class with her for a few days to help her get over her shyness and fear?"

"No, that's not a good idea," said the nun. "We need to get them to be able to function without mommy."

Mary Louise's mother finally pried Mary Louise loose and gave her into the loving hands of Sister Thomas, who brought her over to some other girls who had already said goodbye to their mothers.

"This is Mary Louise," said Sister. "Can she stand with you here?"

The girls looked at the sister in awe and they nodded their heads. Then they looked at Mary Louise and grimaced.

"And who is this handsome young man?" asked Sister Thomas. People who met me always said how good looking I was.

My father nudged me. "I am Francis Scoblete," I said.

"Well, Francis, welcome to Our Lady of Angels. I am sure you are going to like it here."

"Yes," I said. Then my father and mother kissed me and walked away. I waved goodbye then turned my attention to the other kids. In my five years, I had not had many friends to play with so I was interested in these other kids. Some looked like babies and some looked a lot older than I.

Then Sister rang a hand-held bell and we all walked into the school. The classroom had all sorts of books, crayons, paper, displays, a screen, decorations and religious paintings of Christ on the cross and the Virgin Mary floating up into the sky with little angels all around her.

"Boys and girls, we now separate; the girls go over here," she pointed to her right, "and the boys go over there," and she pointed to her left. "We have an even number of boys and an even number of girls so each of you get a partner and we will start with our morning prayer."

Some little boy took my hand, "Can I be your partner?" he asked. "Okay," I said. This little boy looked scared. He was the smallest kid in the class.

Mary Louise was left over because no girl wanted to be her partner and one other girl, a shy one, was also alone. "You two are going to be partners," said Sister happily.

The shy little girl walked to the nun and whispered, "She smells bad."

"She is one of God's children," said Sister Thomas.

"She smells bad," whispered the shy girl.

"You and she are partners," said Sister Thomas more firmly. The shy girl looked over at Mary Louise who seemed redder than before.

"Yes, sister," said the shy girl. I liked the shy girl; she seemed very pleasant and clean-looking in her Catholic school uniform which was a navy blue dress and a white blouse.

"Boys and girls," said Sister Thomas clapping her hands to quiet the few kids who were talking. "Welcome to Our Lady of Angel's kindergarten class. Many of you are scared because this is the first time you have been away from your parents. But this is the first day of the rest of your lives."

Many of the kids lost interest in what Sister was saying because five year-olds don't have much of an attention span and these distracted kids looked around the classroom. I looked at the painting of Jesus with the blood flowing from his head, hands, feet and sides. Strangely enough I had great powers of concentration, even at five.

"We are now going to say our morning prayers," said Sister Thomas. "Everyone stand up." We all stood up. "In the name of the Father and the Son and the Holy Ghost," she made the sign of the cross and we all tried to follow it. "Dear God and his son Jesus, please help our young people to be good Catholics and to pray for the conversion of Russia a land of atheists and killers."

Russia, what was that?

"Amen," she said.

We all looked at her.

"Say Amen," she said.

"Amen," we all said.

Then we had the first day. I don't really remember what we did because it was non-stop action—do this, do that, do this other thing—all designed to keep little kids interested, busy and, to some degree, learning. Some of the kids couldn't really concentrate on anything and there was always one or two or three of them wandering around looking confused. At two hours into the class, Sister Thomas clapped and called everyone to attention. "It is now cookies and milk time, boys and girls," she said.

Some of the kids cheered.

Sister brought out a giant platter of cookies and big containers of milk. She passed out cups to all of us and she went around the room giving out one cookie per student and pouring milk into our cups. "This is what God gives us children," said Sister Thomas over and over.

Mary Louise grabbed three of "God's cookies" off the tray as Sister turned her attention to some other kids who were hitting each other.

Mary Louise quickly gobbled down the three cookies and drained the milk in one giant gulp. Then she saw her shy partner delicately eating her cookie, after dunking it genteelly in her milk, and Mary Louise grabbed it away from her. Mary Louise gobbled that down too. The shy girl was pale and upset but didn't say anything. Mary Louise held her hand out and the shy girl gave Mary Louise her milk, which Mary Louise chugged.

After we enjoyed our repast, Mary Louise started making weird noises—gurgles, a couple of wet farts, and then a white line started at the top of her head and headed down her face— she was changing from a hairy red thing to a hairy white thing. When the white made its way to her chin, Mary Louise made some animal sounds and then projectile-vomited across the entire room: aaaaarrrrgggggghhhhhhh! Glop! Glop! spraying most of the kids in class and landing full-splash on several in the back of the room. Projectile vomit is like a shooting star; the bulk of it heads across the heavens but it has a tail that falls to earth before the bulk of it lands. That tail was puke particles that hit most of us.

I was spared the hit and so was my little partner, but the other kids were screaming and one or two started to vomit on themselves and their partners. Shortly, the Our Lady of Angel's kindergarten class of Sister Thomas Mahoney was a puke-fest with most of the kids letting their cookies and milk explode all over the place.

Mary Louise had hurled her two "vomit comets" (as we ultimately titled them) across the heaven of the class room and she now looked around to find something to eat. She was eyeing the puke but Sister Thomas quickly led everyone to the bathroom where she and several other nuns cleaned the kids off. The only two without any puke particles on them were my little partner and I. Yes, God was good.

After school the mothers congregated outside waiting for their sons and daughters. When the kids came out the mothers hugged them and asked how their day was. The kids told about their exciting adventure of the day—no, not learning. You could now see the mothers looking over at Mary Louise as the first information the mothers received had to do with the vomit comet and its aftermath.

Mary Louise's mother talked to Sister Thomas who went to her even before Mary Louise did. Mary Louise was busy grubbing candy from another mother who had brought some for her son. "More, more," demanded Mary Louise.

"I told you," said Mrs. Roncallo, "that Mary Louise has a delicate stomach and she must be treated very gently, do you understand?"

"Mrs. Roncallo," said Sister Thomas sternly, "she vomited on everyone in the class. Has she been taken to a doctor?"

"The doctor says she is a very special child. She is smart but sensitive."

And that continued all through kindergarten and elementary school. Mary Louise Roncallo on almost all important occasions reacted with vomit.

She had an unusual talent. Like a fine wine, she just got better with age.

2

The Holy Communion
Conundrum

Bless me father for I have sinned.
I booked bets during First Holy Communion.

In second grade, I felt sorry for the poor Protestants who had no idea of what our Holy Communion was all about. Father McCain explained it perfectly. "Boys and girls, only the Catholic Church has the *Truth* with a capital 'T.' Our Holy Communion is a sacrament where the real Jesus Christ exists in the bread that you receive in the Holy Eucharist, which is another name for Holy Communion."

Since we were going to make our First Holy Communion next week, Father McCain had come to the second grade classes to make sure we knew what this sacred event was all about.

"Those poor Protestants think that the giving of the bread and wine is just a symbol, which means it isn't real. No, my young Catholic men and women, the *transubstantiation* which as you all know means that the bread and wine are really changed into the actual body and blood of our Lord Jesus Christ is real. Jesus Christ is fully in each and every Host [bread wafer] that you consume. You are taking Christ into your body to cleanse you and to make you strong spiritual Catholics so if the atheist Communists conquer the world you will have the strength to never deny your religion even if they torture you to death by putting burning spits on your skin, poking out your eyes and cutting off your heads and doing even worse things. Remember that the Communists are the most murderous people on earth."

How could those Communists make their *spit* burning hot? How did they do such a thing? Did they spit in a pot and boil it and then throw it on your exposed skin? What animals those atheists were!

And those poor Protestants, too; they had no idea of the Truth with a capital "T."

"The Communists and the Protestants are all going to Hell," reminded Sister Elise Martin in her stern voice.

"Sister," said Father McCain, and then he broke with the Catholic tradition of that time by saying, "there are some very good Protestants who just don't know any better. God is all merciful and I think some will be saved."

"But *all* the Communists are going to Hell," scolded the sister. *Disagree with that* was her tone.

To forestall a theological argument in front of impressionable minds, Father McCain said, "Oh, yes, *all* the Communists are going to Hell."

"And *most* Protestants," added sister forcefully. Father McCain gave her a look out of the side of his face but he didn't say anything. This nun always wanted the last word and she always got it.

"Father?" asked Joel, one of the two Jewish kids—yes, some Jewish kids were in our school. "If this bread is the body and blood of Jesus when you bite into it does it bleed?"

"No," said Father McCain. "The miracle is that the bread stays bread but is transformed on a real and spiritual level into the body and blood of Christ."

"If you examine the bread then it is still bread?" asked Joel.

"Yes and that is where faith comes in," said the priest.

"The true faith Joel, the *true* faith, not like some others" added Sister Elise Martin.

With these big questions of Jesus Christ in the bread and wine; with Hell dangling over the heads of most people on earth (and on Catholics who sinned), with atheists who could put burning spit on you, many of the girls had religious questions.

"Father," asked the love of my young life, Mary Sissallo, "if we are eating the real body and blood of Jesus Christ does that mean there will only be two people in the Blessed Trinity instead of the Father, the Son, and the Holy Ghost since Jesus is being eaten piece by piece?"

"God's ways are not man's ways," stated the sister.

Mary Sissallo looked confused.

"Sister," said Father McCain, "let me answer the questions, please, as that is my job as a priest."

Sister Elise Martin's face turned tight and she nodded slightly. Most of the boys were delighted that Father McCain had slapped her down. This nun favored the girls. She always told the class that the girls had the fast route to heaven because the mother of Christ was a woman and even though Christ was a man, he was also God which meant that other men were inferior because they were not God. This made sense to her but I had no idea what she was talking about—except I understood that girls had a better chance of going to heaven and boys were in trouble.

"Mary Sissallo," said Father McCain who knew all of our names, "that was a very good question. You used logic to try to understand something that seems impossible—that Jesus could be consumed by man and still exist in other forms at the same time. But that is the power of God, to do the impossible. God created the Universe but He is not subject to the laws of the Universe as we are. He can do all things that He wishes to do even if they seem impossible or illogical to us."

That was as good an explanation as any I had heard even though I had no idea of what it meant. Most of religion made no sense and that is why you needed faith.

"If the Host represents Jesus," said Catherine Elizabeth O'Connor.

"No! No!" jumped in Sister Elise.

Father McCain held up his hand indicating that sister should be quiet.

"Jesus is there fully in the flesh. The Host does not represent Him; it *is* Him."

"I am sorry," said Catherine, adjusting her thick glasses. "Here is my question, Father. What if the Host falls to the floor?

"Since the Host is the sacred body of the Most High, Jesus Christ, the priest is the only one who can pick it up off the floor. No one else can touch the Host, only a consecrated Catholic priest."

Now you would think that at this stage in our development the boys too would be in awe of the sacrament we were about to receive, and in some ways I guess we were. It was, after all, an absolutely amazing thing to be eating Jesus Christ Himself. But we had other concerns; much more immediate practical concerns that were far easier to understand and took up more of our mental time.

Oh yes, there was a BIG other thing in our minds, Big with a capital "B," which overshadowed everything Father McCain was telling us.

I was nominated by head-nodding acclimation to ask the BIG question.

"Father, if someone pukes . . ." All eyes immediately turned to Mary Louise Roncallo, who had puked enough times since kindergarten to make us fully aware that First Holy Communion could be an amazing stage for a spectacular performance by the vomit-comet queen.

"That is disgusting, Francis," yelled sister aiming her deadly eyes at me.

Riding right over her, Father McCain said, "Yes, Francis, if such a thing happens, and it has never happened in my thirty years in the priesthood so don't worry, the priest would have to take the elements of the Host out of the, ah, uh, stuff."

The only ones who didn't know we were talking about Mary Louise were Father McCain and Mary Louise herself. Mary Louise didn't seem too self aware or she wouldn't eat like a hippopotamus, often bullying to steal the other kids' food. She would do this to the smaller kids who were afraid of her massive hairy body; she would loom over them until they sheepishly handed over their sandwiches, cookies and pies; and she would also steal food from the tougher kids when they weren't looking as she had lightning-fast hands when it came to food.

Mary Louise Roncallo seemed the size of a horse; had the appetite of an elephant and the hygiene of a pig, and she was now fully coated with small black hairs all over her reddish skin.

"So," I continued in order to make sure I had this exactly right. "If you were the priest and someone puked all over the place . . ."

"Francis Scoblete!" shouted the sister. Father McCain put his hand up to silence her again.

"Yes, if I were the priest that is what I would have to do. It is one of the Laws of the Church."

So for the next week the boys set up a notebook guessing at what time in the First Holy Communion Mass Mary Louise would let loose. I figured she'd launch sometime after receiving the body and blood of Our Lord, Jesus Christ. Up until then her stomach would be empty since we were supposed to fast from after dinner on Friday evening until we ate Christ at Saturday's First Holy Communion ceremony. Since there were 23 boys in the class, the times were spread out all over the place.

All the girls, except for Theresa Blodgett, refused to participate in our lottery because it was disrespectful to the Lord Jesus Christ, Himself. I tried to explain to some of the girls that the Lord wasn't the issue; it was Mary Louise. The girls disdained me. Maybe Sister Elise Martin was right after all; girls were better than boys.

The big day finally arrived.

My mother dressed me in the special First Holy Communion suit with a carnation in the lapel. The girls all wore white dresses to symbolize that they never got dirty. I didn't realize at the time that the white dress symbolized that they were marrying Jesus Christ. When I was told that a few months later I said, "I thought Jesus Christ never got married?" Later I was told that being the bride of Christ was not what marrying Jesus really meant. These nuns could drive you crazy with their "it means that but it really doesn't mean that" routines. After awhile I just shut my ears—and that made Catholic life a lot easier to handle. It could drive you crazy knowing that everything that was was also everything that wasn't.

The nuns lined all the classes up in Our Lady of Angels school yard, with the girls on one side and the boys on the other, each group forming their Holy Communion line. We were lined up in height order; the smallest boy, Hugo Twaddle, first, all the way to the two giants of our class, Kenny Peterson and the towering Patrick Heelan being the last two. I was in the middle of the line.

The girls were lined up with itsy-bitsy Maria De Cardinale first and the humongous Mary Louise Roncallo last.

The parents filled the massive Our Lady of Angels church, which was on Fourth Ave between 73rd and 74th Streets. Once all the parents were inside, the organist began the music and we were slowly ushered into the massive church.

If you faced the altar, the boys were seated on the left side of the church; the girls were seated on the right. Nuns patrolled the aisles, making sure no one talked as this was, as one nun reverently put it, "Your entrance into Life Everlasting through your own free will given to mankind at the dawn of creation when we were perfect but made all the wrong choices from then on." That seemed formidable . . . whatever it meant.

As we entered the church the shortest kids were seated in the front rows; the tallest kids in the last rows. A couple of parents dared to take pictures in the church as the procession entered and they were quickly tongue-lashed by the nuns nearest them. "This is a house of God!" loudly proclaimed Sister Elise. "Not a photography studio!" Since Our Lady of Angels was a huge church anything that was said, even when whispered, would echo. So everyone in the church could hear sister's admonishment echoing throughout the building. "NOT A PHOTOGRAPHY STUDIO! NOT A PHOTOGRAPHY STUDIO! NOT A PHOTOGRAPHY STUDIO! NOT A PHOTOGRAPHY STUDIO!"

The boys and girls had somber expressions on their faces. This was not the time for levity, even when Ladislav Hamlin ripped a rather loud and disgustingly smelly fart. We ignored it, except for a couple of giggles from some of the boys. Every girl completely ignored it even though it could be heard and then smelled for quite a distance. All the girls had their heads bowed—God were they religious.

Once we were all seated, Father McCain and several altar boys entered the altar area and the Mass began. In those days the Mass was said in Latin which sounded mystical and the priest faced the altar so no one could quite see what he was doing. That made the Mystery of the Transubstantiation even greater since it was all so secretive.

Father McCain gave a sermon about the importance of the Holy Eucharist in the life of a Catholic because it was our chance to share in the mystery of the Holy Trinity and the Life of God Himself.

Then it was time for us to eat Jesus Christ, the Lord, Himself. The nuns went from row to row indicating when it was our turn to go into the center aisle, our hands in prayer mode, and then we walked slowly and solemnly to the Communion railing. Since Mary Louise was behind me I wasn't able to see her until I came back from being given a dry, tasteless wafer which I was not allowed to chew—Christ had to melt in your mouth, like M&Ms. As soon as I had that bread in my mouth I committed a little blasphemy when I thought, "Christ doesn't taste too good."

Coming back to my pew, there was Mary Louise passing me going to the Communion rail—her face as red as blood. I could see those little heaves starting that if left unchecked would result in horror for all around her and a win for the kid who picked the right time.

I was already seated in my pew, kneeling, supposedly praying to Jesus, and the Father and the Holy Ghost, but I was actually watching the monstrous Mary standing after receiving the Host. She turned to walk back to her pew. Now the white line showed on her forehead. The boys gasped in excitement. The MOMENT was at hand!

Mary started to make her gurgles, "ugh, ah, urp, urp, blurf, yorg" as she slowly headed back to the last pew. The girls in front of her were now very much aware that danger was in the offing as they heard the prelude, "ugh, ah, urp, urp, blurf, yorg," and so they started to walk faster to put some distance between themselves and her, knowing full well that with the projectile vomit of Mary Louise there was really no escaping if the comet headed towards them or over them. With that arcing vomit-comet doom looming, you'd get some, most or almost all of it on yourself and everything around you. It was fate; like Christ having to be hung on the cross to save the rest of us from bad things. It was the way of the world.

The adults started to look at her as the white line now covered her face from forehead to nose. You could see some of the adults pointing, "What is that dear? On that kid?" "I have no idea, honey."

Loud: "Ugh, ah, urp, urp, blurf, yorg!" You could hear it echoing in the church. *"Ugh, ah, urp, urp, blurf, yorg." "Ugh, ah, urp, urp, blurf, yorg." "Ugh, ah, urp, burp, blurf, yorg."*

Sister Elise turned towards Mary and stopped in her tracks. The nuns all knew of Mary's puking prowess and none of them wanted to get in the way either.

Louder: "Ugh! Ah! Urp! Urp! Blurf! Yorg!" (*Echo, Echo, Echo.*) All heads turned towards Mary Louise Roncallo.

"It's coming!" I whispered to Arman Carmen Buddy Frasca the Third.

Loud as all Hell: "UGH! AH! URP! URP! BLURF! YORG!" (*Echo! Echo! Echo!*)

Mary Louise's head started to sway from one side to the other. Her face was now totally white. Her mustache was highlighted prominently. The girls ahead of her were now sprinting to get away. The boys' side of the church were all ducking and praying she wouldn't turn in our direction. The parents looked befuddled.

And then:"Arrrrrrrrrrrrrrrrrrroooooooooooooouuuuuuuuggggggg ghhhhhh!!!!! Arrrrrrrrrrrroooooooooouuuuuuuugggggggghhhhhhh!!!!!!!" and a HUGE (with a capital 'H-U-G-E') vomit-comet rocketed up out of her mouth and sailed majestically up over the pews where the adults were sitting stunned. As the comet dripped on them small multi-colored pink gobs of whatever had been in Mary Louise's stomach, the comet made its descent into the pews where even more parents sat in wide-eyed awe as the comet landed and splashed gallons of stinking goo all over them.

From the altar I saw Father McCain quickly turn around, look in bewilderment as the sounds of hundreds of attendees echoed in the church.

McCain saw the vomit-comet splash its contents over pews and pews of his beloved church floor, and the kneeling parents and other parishioners and (God save him) he yelled (without thinking mind you of his role as a servant priest of the Almighty God) he yelled right from the altar: "OH, SHIT!" which echoed all over the church, *"Ohhhhhhh Shiiiiiit! Ohhhhhhh Shiiiiiit! Ohhhhhhh Shiiiiiit!"* to the bug-eyed astonishment of all the adults and First Holy Communion recipients.

The parents who had been baptized in the gooey gobs from Mary Louise fled the church uttering low screams; wives and grandmas weeping into their handkerchiefs. All their new clothes had been drenched in dreck. Other adults held their noses as they tried to act unconcerned but they quickly fled the church too. A few of the other kids puked too as Mary Louise had lofted a Godzilla-like blob that smelled like the bodies burned in the never-ending fires of Hell itself. It was hard not to puke. Even I fought the urge.

"That was great," said Jake "the Snake" Jacobsen.

"That was an atomic bomb!" smiled Billy Bell.

"I think I hit it on the head when she'd do it," said Steve Gardell.

The stern-faced nuns escorted us all out, by rows, in an orderly fashion, and we went into the schoolyard, still in height order.

I could imagine poor Father McCain going through all that puke when everyone left the church looking for pieces of Jesus' body. It wasn't easy being a priest in the Catholic Church.

In the schoolyard as we were about to split up and look for our parents, Mary Louise said, "I'm hungry," and stared at the smaller girls.

3

Father Has
A Condition!

Bless me father for I have sinned. I insulted a priest.

Depending on your grades in the various subjects, Our Lady of Angels had a wonderful or brutal way to give out report cards to the kids every 10 weeks—that ten-week period of terror for the dopes, of which I was one, or ecstasy for the really smart kids. Father Haggerty, the priest in charge of the schools, came in and handed out the report cards. He looked them over and made comments. The cards were arranged with the kids having the highest marks called up first.

Father Haggerty had one little problem. He was a drunkard; a sprawling, splaying, at times slightly drooling drunkard. Sister Mary Michaels, our fourth-grade teacher, never said as such since that would be disrespectful to a man of the "claws" (at least that's what I heard). She said he had a "condition" when kids asked her about Father Haggerty staggering around in the yard between the school and our magnificent church or leaning up against the fence to get his balance.

Father Haggerty had wispy white hair, a big red face with a multi-colored pocked nose like W.C. Fields, and a stern countenance—except he bumped into walls, tripped over things, including his own feet, and mumbled when he was really soused.

When Mary Louise Roncallo asked Sister Mary Michaels if Father Haggerty was a drunk, Sister Mary displayed anger at Mary Louise.

"No, young lady, Father Haggerty is not a drunk. He has a *condition!*" shouted Sister Mary. "He has a condition that we should pray for."

"My father has that condition," said Mary Louise, "and my mother says he's a drunk."

"No, young lady, no."

Upset, Mary Louise was starting to have that white line go down her forehead. If you caught a glimpse of her face, you knew what was coming soon. All the kids now knew the symptoms and signs of an impending explosion. And we had to stop it now. If you could catch the line before it went under her eyes, you could prevent the Roncallo vomit-comet.

"Well that is all good and all . . ." started Beanie Lynch.

"Young man," said Sister Mary, turning her full attention to him. "You did not raise your hand."

Beanie immediately raised his hand, so did I, and so did just about every boy in the class. Most of the girls were not as forceful in those innocent days and only a few had timidly put up their hands.

"What is going on here?" asked Sister Mary.

"We want to discuss this," said Joe Romano.

"Father Haggerty is a man of God and a person who shows us the way to heaven as our Lord and Master Jesus Christ wished," scolded Sister Mary.

At the moment we didn't care if Father Haggerty could fly and simultaneously fart snowflakes; we had to completely get the attention away from Mary Louise Roncallo who could make this, as she had so often, a very unpleasant day.

"I am an altar boy and he loads up the chalice to the top with wine and he doesn't put any water in, he just pretends to," said Ben Smith.

"That is not true," said Sister Mary.

"Yes it is," said Ben.

"No, it isn't," said Sister Mary, "and to say that is a violation of the Ten Commandments about bearing false witness."

That one threw us. What was she talking about?

I glanced over at Mary Louise and, thank God and the Blessed Virgin herself, Mary Louise's face went back to its natural red color under her facial hair.

So when Father Haggerty staggered in to give us our report cards we ignored the fact that he dropped some of them and then walked into Sister Mary Michael's desk.

Then my slow agony began. I wasn't the stupidest kid in the class; I was about the third stupidest.

Father Haggerty started:

"Mary Sissallo, another outstanding report card. You have a hundred in almost every subject, including religion! You are a role model of a young Catholic girl."

Mary, my first love and the unfortunate object of my disastrous virgin kiss (see my book *The Virgin Kiss*) blushed and went to the front to get her card. Father shook her hand as he handed her the report card.

"Hugo Twaddle, you are almost as good as Mary. You are a fine Catholic young man."

"Herb Bernstein, another one-hundred percent in religion! Congratulations." Then he looked over at the rest of us. "Aren't the rest of you ashamed that one of the three one-hundreds in religion in a class of fifty Catholics is to a *Jewish* kid? He's doing his work and you aren't! His parents are proud of him and your parents think you are jerks."

Herb Bernstein beamed because he knew his parents were proud of him—after all he was the third smartest kid in the class—and one of the two Jews; the other Jewish kid was the eighth smartest kid in the class. In those golden Bay Ridge days, some Jewish parents sent their kids to Our Lady of Angels because of how good the education was and how awful it was in the local public schools.

When Father Haggerty castigated the rest of the class we tried not to meet his wet-red gaze.

And he continued until he got to me. By this time I was a nervous wreck.

"Ah, Francis Scobolet . . ."

"Sco-blet-ee," I corrected.

"Young man, quiet please," said Sister Mary Michael. "Do not interrupt the father."

"But he always gets my name wrong," I countered.

"Quiet," said Sister.

"That is okay my dear Sister because the arrogance of this young thug . . .

"Thug?" I asked.

"Only thugs answer priests back," spouted Father Haggerty, spit flying out of his mouth, and drool now rolling down his chin.

"I wasn't answering you back," I said. "I was just telling you how my name is pronounced. You always mispronounce it, Father."

"Because with your grades," he looked at my report card. "You shouldn't have a name." Then he paused and his eyes swelled up. "My Lord, young man, you have a twelve in religion! A twelve! My Lord of Hosts!"

Maybe it was because I was so wound up but I countered. "I wanted to honor the twelve apostles."

There was a pause and then the class erupted with laughter. Since I was a kind of funny kid I smiled at that line. I got a 12 in religion because *I wanted to honor the 12 apostles.* That was a great line! *That* was also a *great* mistake.

"You should be tarred and feathered!" screamed Haggerty. "You deserve to be beaten to within an inch of your miserable life."

"I didn't do anything wrong, I just failed religion," I said.

"Just? *Just?*" screamed Father Haggerty. "A boiling ash-filled heaping burning mound awaits you in Hell! Burning spits will agonize you!" What was it with those burning spits? You kept being told about them. Who kept burning their spits?

"I am not going to Hell!" I screamed back, although a part of me knew that Father Haggerty might be right. I was committing mortal sins of indecent actions on myself like crazy by that time.

"You are Hell bound!" he screamed. Sister Mary Michaels nodded her head sagely. Obviously it was common knowledge that I was Hell bound.

I had had it by then.

"And you're a drunk!" I yelled at Father Haggerty. The class was in shock, except for the stupid kids who guffawed at my witty attack on the priest.

"You're a drunk!" I screamed at the top of my lungs. But no one could scream like Sister Mary Michaels.

"He is *not* a drunk!" screamed Sister Mary Michaels. "He has a *condition!* He has a *condition!* You horrible little boy!"

She grabbed her ever-ready strap and bolted down the aisle to the back of the class where the stupid kids were seated and she started whaling on me.

"He is not a drunk!" Whap on top of my head. "He has a *condition!*" Wham to the back of the head as I tried to duck. "A condition!" Wham, whop, bam, all over my head, cheeks, and neck. She was really getting into it now.

Father Haggerty had staggered down the aisle and took her hand just before she launched another attack on me. "Leave him Sister," he said gently. Sister Mary Michaels looked at him. "Let God handle him," said Father Haggerty. Sister put down her strap, gave me an ugly look, and said, "Francis Scoblete, I expect to see your parents tomorrow morning before school starts," and she walked back to the front of the class. I knew I was now in even bigger trouble because my parents would be told of my damnation.

In all the confusion, Valentine Zumwalt and Stephen Godowsky's report cards were not read out loud. They had both failed every subject and were on the verge of being thrown out of school and sent to the neighborhood public school—a fate almost as bad as the fate of the Hell bound.

The three of us were indeed suffering; two about to be jettisoned from Our Lady of Angels into (horrors!) public school and me, the worst of our trinity, going to Hell.

I should have known better than to attack a man of the "claws."

4

I Lost Some Seeds

Bless me father for I have sinned. I did you-know-what.

Going to weekly confession was a horrifying practice that the Catholic schools inflicted on us when we were kids. But it was the only way to get us to Mass on Sunday with relatively few sins on our immortal souls. Saturday afternoon confession; Sunday Holy Communion and the rest of the week we added loads of sins to our souls' account book. (Please note: the boys had whole *books* of sins, some of us had whole *volumes*, but the girls only had little booklets according to the nuns.)

There were so many sins to remember, most of them important enough that you had better confess them or you were then committing a *double* sin—the sin itself that you forgot to confess and the sin of omission for not confessing it. The Church had you coming and going.

The Our Lady of Angels' nuns, the Sisters of Charity, delighted in taking us to the hardest priests (so much for "charity"), the meanest of which was that weasel-faced Father Sullivan. If he were "on duty," then the nuns happily dragged the boys over to him.

Of course, the nuns took the girls to the easiest priest, Father Eckert, who knew very little English since he was German and sounded like those dirty Nazis in the movies. But he was good looking according to the girls and they loved to go to confession with him. While Sullivan gave massive penance—"You will say the rosary ten times, boy,"—the girls usually got in broken English, "Pleez say von Heil Mary, yung laady, and alzo pray for de convershun of zee soulz in Ruesha."

"You boys are bigger sinners than the girls," explained Sister Jerome Drake nodding knowingly and glaring savagely at Valentine Zumwalt who had asked why we had to go to Father Sullivan when the girls got off easy. "You have to go to a priest who understands the *nature* of your sins. The girls don't have to worry about *that*. They have different natures. They have better natures because a woman was the mother of God."

None of the boys looked at Sister Jerome Drake when she talked about "the nature of your sins" because we were all thinking of what the nature of our greatest sin was—a sin we all shared in common, day after day after day, night after night after night, a sin we were obsessed with—which was, to put it mildly—a sin called "self abuse." Or "impure thoughts with actions."

Of course, when you went to confession to Father Sullivan, "the terror of the tingolators," it didn't matter if you confessed to "self-abuse," or "impure thoughts and actions," or "doing something bad with my male part," he knew what you meant and he mercilessly hammered you about the *nature* of your sin. Evidently girls didn't have those parts, although for the life of me I couldn't figure out what kind of part they had instead.

So now we were sitting in the pews waiting for our turn to enter the confessional with the fiery Father Sullivan. In the confessional was Eugene O'Toole, a really tough kid who had never lost a street fight, and suddenly the booming voice of Father Sullivan could be heard echoing throughout the massive Our Lady of Angels church and causing the girls to look over at the "boys' section" of the church with shock and horror, "You did what!? You did WHAT!?" (*What!? What!?* echoing throughout the church.) Then silence.

Probably O'Toole was whispering, trying to come up with a way to decrease the severity of his sin, begging the priest not to scream at him again. That's what we all did. We all tried to make it as if what it was, it really wasn't *that*, but something else all together. Nothing ever worked. "You did *what!?*" was Father Sullivan's mantra, one that could be heard across the George Washington Bridge going to New Jersey.

When O'Toole left the confessional, he was red as a beet and I could see that O'Toole's face seemed to be swollen and pumping like a heart. He couldn't look directly at the rest of us who also couldn't look directly at him out of embarrassment for him and, more important, for what awaited us—which was the exact same explosion from Father Sullivan as O'Toole got. Of course, none of us wanted to admit to our fellow sinners just what our sin was even though we all knew what it was nevertheless.

I turned to my friend Arman Carmen Buddy Frasca the Third and said, "I think I know how to get around this. I think I've got it."

"How?" he asked excited.

"I'm not going to tell you until I see how it works . . . but I know it will work. I've been thinking about this all week." I pointed to my head as if to say *In here is the brain that will defeat Father Sullivan.*

And I had. I knew all the tried and true methods of how we tried to talk our way around this "thing we did" and try to diminish it even though we did it every day and/or night during the week from Sunday evening through to Saturday afternoon's confession. None of these methods of excuse ever worked. But I'd hit old Father Sullivan with something he had never heard of before but which meant the same thing and I would get a light confession, "Say a Hail Mary, young man, and good for you for not having too many sins and for overcoming your nature."

I'd be able to look over at the girls, smug in my knowledge that I had told the truth, got a light penance like they did, without Father Sullivan being the wiser.

You see, I had convinced myself that it wasn't a sin if Father Sullivan didn't know what I was really talking about. If I had told it in my own words, then it was his job to understand what I was saying, right? I couldn't be held responsible before the throne of God for the ignorance of one of his priests, could I? Of course not!

Jake "the Snake" Jacobsen came out of his side of the confessional, pale as a ghost, and lumbered to the altar where you had to say your penance. O'Toole was still there too, kneeling and trying to get it all over with. The good thing about confession, maybe the only good thing, was the fact that once you were down near the altar, kneeling, saying your penance, you were joined by dozens of your fellow classmates. The boys' side of the altar was packed with us saying our penances. The girl's side had one or two who would quickly finish and be replaced by one or two more who also quickly finished. If church had been a boat, it would have capsized because all the weight was on the boys' side of the deck.

It was now my turn. I was supremely confident.

If you aren't Catholic you might not know how the confessionals had been constructed. It was a big closet with the priest sitting in the middle with a wall on either side of him. On the other side of the wall were the victims, or as the Catholic Church called them—the penitents—and the priest would slide a little square wooden door, maybe a foot wide, high and long, between you and him, and then he would hear your confession. Supposedly he couldn't see you through the screen that separated you and him, but most of us believed that he could, in fact, see very clearly and he knew exactly who you were as you told him the "nature" of your sins.

Father Sullivan slid the door open between us.

"Yes?" he said.

"Bless me father for I have sinned. It has been one week since my last confession. I was not nice to my sister Susan four times, I disobeyed my mother six times, I disobeyed my father once and he belted me in the head, I lost some seeds, I didn't pay attention in class five times, I teased Patricia Conway four times, I stayed up past my bedtime and watched Million Dollar Movie on television by sneaking to the door when my parents thought I was asleep."

I knew I had the right cadence going—all sins equally presented. I slipped in the "I lost some seeds," casually, right in the middle of all my other sins.

There was a pause. I kept thinking, *give me the penance; give me the penance.*

"What do you mean you lost some seeds?" asked Father Sullivan.

"I, uh, I lost some seeds," I said.

"Yes, but what do you mean?"

"Seeds," I said.

"I know you said seeds. What kind of seeds?"

"Just seeds," I said.

"Like rose seeds?"

"Uh, no, uh, not rose seeds," I said.

"Explain to me what kind of seeds you are talking about."

"There are all kinds of seeds," I said and I thought, *I can't lie my way out of this in confession, I'll go to Hell if I get hit by that bus.*

Non-Catholics don't know about THE BUS, so let me take a pause to explain.

The kindly Sisters of Charity of Our Lady of Angels all told us the story about THE BUS that came from nowhere that killed those who had committed mortal sins. There were two types of sin in Catholicism, venial sins and mortal sins. Venial sins were small sins that could not condemn you to the eternal raging fires of Hell. Mortal sins were serious offenses against the laws of God and if you died with one of those on your soul you went straight to the eternal fire. Mortal sins included murder and missing Mass on Sunday.

When the story was told in fifth grade THE BUS usually ran over any boy or girl who had kissed a member of the opposite sex, which was considered a mortal sin in fifth grade. I'm guessing that if you kissed a member of the same sex a whole fleet of Greyhound buses turned you into mush right on 3rd Avenue but none of us even knew about that type of kissing.

The nuns told us that the two of them, the boy and the girl, had kissed and as they were walking home THE BUS came at them and killed one or the other of them, and the remaining living one had to live with the knowledge for the rest of his or her life that he or she had sent the other person to their eternal damnation in the fiery pit of Satan. That was some burden to carry and so when you were in a state of mortal sin, which just about every boy was just about every day except for the hours between Saturday afternoon's confession and Sunday morning's Mass, that bus loomed in your life. We were all extremely careful crossing the avenues that had bus traffic.

So if I lied to Father Sullivan's interrogation in confession I would be adding another mortal sin to my other mortal sin of losing some seeds. THE BUS hit then would be doubly bad.

"I am waiting for an explanation of what kind of seeds you are talking about," said Father Sullivan impatiently.

I gave it one last effort at concealment without overtly lying. "All things start with seeds, Father," I said.

"You masturbated," he said firmly.

"Uh, ah, ooo, uh, oh, uh, eh," I stammered.

"You were trying to pull one over on me with this seed business!" he screamed.

"I, uh, ah, eh, oh," I stammered.

"My God, you beast, you did WHAT!?" he screamed and I could hear that scream echoing throughout the church because Our Lady of Angel's huge edifice was an echoing mountain valley.

"Father I uh, ah, eh . . . ."

"You just drove big fat nails into Christ's hands which are now spurting blood all over the cross and on his mother the Blessed Virgin Mary who is crying her tears for the sins of people like you! You've driven a spear into our Lord's side now and the blood is dripping down his legs. You have crucified the Lord your God who is now dying on the cross because you lied in confession about seeds. Seeds!" he screamed and I could hear the word "seeds" echoing in the church. *SEEDS, SEEDS, SEEDS, SEEDS . . . .*

"Ooo, ah, eee," I said.

"For your penance, you must say the rosary five times!" he screamed. I was about to say the closing prayer when he stopped me. "One last thing, boy."

"Ya, ya, yes?"

"How many times do you think you lost these seeds?"

"Twice a day."

For the rest of my grammar school career I had to keep a sharp eye out for THE BUS. I knew its license plate had my name on it.

5

My Religious Vocation

Bless me father for I have sinned. I failed in my attempt to be a priest.

At some time or other every Catholic school kid figures that God is calling him or her to the religious orders. I was no different. In fifth grade, for a single week, I thought God was calling me to be a priest.

I liked that image of me, a man of God, peaceful, loving his fellow man, helping humanity become better than the sinful beasts they actually were.

So I got my rosary beads and connected them to my belt and let them hang down my leg to show every student and all the passers-by of Bay Ridge, Brooklyn that this student of Our Lady of Angels grammar school, Francis Scoblete, had been called by the Highest Power in the universe to be one of His own. Look at me; I am God's beloved child ready to serve His desires. I could see the glances that people gave me as I walked through the neighborhood in my holy way with my rosary beads flip-flapping around my thighs. Yes, I was already giving a good example of what it meant to be a future man of the "claws."

I knew that being a Catholic priest could be difficult as there were Communists and Protestants everywhere in America, even in the White House, on television and in the Post Office. But I would persevere, as I had persevered when I had given up television for Lent and then "The Million Dollar Movie" on Channel 9 showed *King*

Kong every night for a week! I had only watched it three nights because of my devotion to my Lenten vow of not watching television at all.

It was during this time that one of the neighborhood's bullies, a public school student, dirty-faced, raggedy but vicious as a werewolf decided now was the time to pick on me. His name was Ferguson and he was really tough. His sister Bonnie was even tougher, although she was two years older than he.

Ferguson had been thrown out of Our Lady of Angels in third grade for failing every single subject and being a real idiot in his behavior. He goosed girls in the coatroom although, truthfully, I never heard any goose sounds coming from there.

It was my first day of my vocation and Ferguson was standing on the corner of 72nd Street and Third Avenue by the mailbox in front of McGuire's bar.

"Hey, shithead!" he yelled at me. He was smoking a cigarette. Obviously his mother didn't care whether he smoked or not because they lived right over the bar and all she had to do was look out the window to see him puffing away. Since Mrs. Ferguson also spent a lot of time *in* the bar, she could have seen Ferguson through the bar's windows too. Ferguson's father was in prison for a series of store burglaries. Ferguson was proud of that.

"My father is the toughest guy in Attica," he'd say with his chest puffing out of his filthy shirt. There was a kind of moldy smell to him.

"Hey, dickman, what's with the rosary beads? You becoming a nun?" he screamed.

Being a peace-loving man of the Good Book, I nodded and smiled a beatific smile. "I am becoming a priest," I said. He walked up to me. "A fucking priest?" he asked.

I continued walking and he left me alone. I was only a block away from my home, which was at Ovington Ave (70th Street) and 3rd Avenue. I spent that night praying and reading comic books and trying not to think about how much fun it would be to lose some seeds.

The next day on my way home, Ferguson was again at the mail box, smoking his cigarette.

"Hey, hey, it's the priest! You fuck!"

"I am a man of God," I nodded to him as I held my rosary beads in my hand. "May God bless you."

"Fuck God! There ain't no God, you asshole," said Ferguson.

Heaven help me, Ferguson was an atheist! He might even be a Communist because they were atheists too. He was going straight to Hell if he were to be hit by THE BUS.

"You should not deny God," I said forcefully and Ferguson punched me in the mouth. I staggered. He punched me again and I went hard against the mail box.

He punched me a third time on the temple and I kind of went to one knee. He stopped punching me then. "You don't fight, you dick?"

"I am a man of God," I said, blood starting to drip out of my mouth, and Ferguson punched me again, this time in the nose, which exploded with blood spraying out and then down on my white Our Lady of Angels shirt.

Ferguson then walked away, taking puffs of his cigarette. "Fuck you, you sissy."

That night I had a decision to make. I really wanted to be a priest but at the same time I didn't want to get beaten up every time I came home from school. I hadn't counted on this kind of martyrdom at the hands of some smelly, scruffy, atheist, burning spit (whatever the heck that was), Communist public-school bully.

Should I throw aside my vocation and fight Ferguson? Or should I stick to my vocation and get my ass kicked every day for the rest of my life?

If I fought Ferguson, it would be the third fight in my life. I didn't think of myself as very tough.

My first fight was with Valentine Zumwalt, a yellow-toothed kid with worse breath than my great uncle Fred, a kid who kept blowing his stench into my face in second grade, "Hiiiiiiiii!" he would say into my nose. I asked him a million times to stop blowing his breath up my nose and his response was always, "Hiiiiiiiii!" right into my nose.

Finally I pushed him. "You wanna fight, huh?" he yelled. "You wanna fight?" What could I do with all the boys and girls now riveted to our dispute?

"Yeah, yeah, I'll fight you!" I said with as much bravado as a second grader could muster.

"After school today, outside Grossman's Soda Fountain," said Zumwalt.

"Yeah, yeah, I'll be there," I said right into his stinking mouth. That damn mouth of his seemed to always be near my nose.

Unfortunately for me, I had never had a fight in my life. What was I going to do?

It was early spring, still with a nip in the air, when I came up with "the" plan. The first rule of fighting, I conjectured, was not to get hurt. If he punched me in the face that would hurt me. How could I prevent that?

I went home at lunchtime and got my winter hat with the thick wool padding inside; with the big padded ear flaps too.

We met outside of Grossman's Soda Fountain.

"Just fists," said Eugene O'Toole, the toughest kid on earth.

Zumwalt and I nodded. Then I put on my hat and made like a boxer, and Zumwalt threw a punch. I ducked and he hit the top of my head. I barely felt it. Then I put up my fists in front of my face and with my head down, I allowed Valentine Zumwalt to whale away at me, hitting me all over the top of my head, thoroughly protected by my makeshift headgear.

Finally Zumwalt stopped. I looked up at him. He hadn't landed one punch on my face. I wasn't hurt. I felt pretty good.

"Had enough?" I asked.

Zumwalt was breathing heavily. He nodded. He was too tired to punch me anymore. That ended my first fisticuffs. But a tactic that worked in second grade wouldn't work with Ferguson who'd probably throw me to the ground and stomp on me. A fifth grader is a lot tougher than a second grader.

As I drifted off to sleep I semi-consciously decided to let matters settle themselves. The next day I headed home from school, rosary beads dangling from my belt and there he was, by the mailbox, in front of McGuire's Bar, Ferguson, smoking and sneering at me. My nose had been hurting me all day since he landed that shot on it yesterday but now it seemed to be throbbing like crazy.

"Hey, priest, ha! ha!" laughed Ferguson. He walked up to me and ripped my rosary beads right off the belt and many of the beads went flying as the chain broke. So, throwing aside being one of God's Emissaries on earth, and instead of turning my other cheek to him, metaphorically speaking, I punched him with all my might right on his cheek. He staggered back and then gained his footing and lunged at me. I backed up and he landed on the pavement, skidding and scrapping his hands so much that they started to bleed.

I jumped on his back and punched him in the back of the neck. He got up like a dog with me on his back. I wrapped my legs around his belly and rode him as if he were a horse. I kept hitting him in the back of the head. My hand was starting to hurt.

He jerked me hard into the mail box and I lost my grip on him. I sprang away and he rose up. His nose was bleeding as were the palms of his hands. He came at me again. Jesus, he was one tough atheist!

I remembered what my father had said about Rocky Marciano. "Frankie, he hit you with short punches. Instead of backing up, he'd come in with a short punch with all his power behind it. Those short punches hurt more than those long looping punches."

So Ferguson lunged forward. I guess he was used to other kids backing up when he did this because his punch was a real roundhouse which would have caught me flush in the face had I been backing up. But I wasn't backing up. I came forward, really fast, and caught him with a short right hand, right on the jaw, and with my knuckles stinging in agony, I saw Ferguson stagger backward. I was startled. I had really hurt him.

I also knew I had better hit him again before he recovered his senses. I stepped forward and hit him with another right hand on the chin. God that hurt—*me!* He came forward and I threw out a left that hit him in the throat and that was all for Ferguson. He stopped. It was as if I weren't there. He shook his head and tried to get his breath.

I went at him again and pushed him into the mailbox. He was really weak since those shots to the jaw and the left to the throat. I tried to mail his head by opening the mailbox but I couldn't quite get his head inside it, although I did get some great kicks into his private parts.

Then two powerful hands grabbed the back of my shirt and lifted me away. I thought maybe some adult from the bar had come out to stop these two kids from killing each other. It wasn't. It was Bonnie Ferguson. *I'm a dead man,* I thought.

"He's finished," said Bonnie. "It's over." She looked at me. That girl could have wiped up the street with me. I knew that. She knew that. "Go home," she said. "He won't bother you again."

I didn't need any more encouragement. I started down the avenue towards home.

I heard Bonnie yelling at her brother but I didn't catch the words because I was so intent on getting away from her—*fast.*

But she was right, Ferguson never bothered me again. Sure, we saw each other now and then and we'd stare at each other but nothing ever came of it. He was never at the mailbox when I came home from school from that fight onward.

Of course, that fight with Ferguson ended my vocational call into the Catholic priesthood. It was just too hard to turn the other cheek and much easier to hit the other guy's cheek.

Religion isn't as easy as many people make it out to be.

6

Justin Goes to Heaven

Bless me father for I have sinned.
I never felt guilt about my teacher's death.

At our Lady of Angels grammar school, teachers rarely retired. Moldy and ancient Franciscan brothers and stooped and desiccated Sisters of Charity worked alongside young, starry-eyed novices in an attempt to instill a good Catholic education into the barbarians they had to teach. Of course, with a few exceptions, most of us barbarians didn't care about a Catholic education per se, or any education for that matter, we just did what we did because that is what you did.

Who knew anything else? The world for us was Catholic and then "all those other people." Some of those "other people" went to our school as well—a couple of Jews, a couple of Protestants too. These kids were okay because, well, they were in our world.

Brother Justin was my sixth-grade teacher. In sixth grade, Our Lady of Angels wisely separated the boys from the girls. The girls stayed with the nuns and the boys, now reaching puberty and the dizzying madness of a monstrously growing libido and other things, went to the men. Oh, and those Franciscan brothers, the young ones, were men's men, for sure. They all participated in the church's sports programs and many of them were awe-inspiringly good athletes. You didn't mess with those young Franciscans, that's for sure.

But many of the older *other* brothers were the walking dead.

Brother Justin, an 89-year-old hunched-backed walking stick, with a face like the crags on a mountainside, along with quivering lips below a mesmerizing facial tick, taught me in the sixth grade. He was the first male teacher I ever had.

Brother Justin was a task master; a man who enjoyed torturing and punishing us when he "caught" us doing something wrong. He was the teacher who called us "barbarians" and said, "You are the reason that Rome fell!" I didn't understand how Rome fell since that was where the Pope was wasn't it? Wasn't Rome still there too? We barbarians looked it up on a map and Rome was still there as far as we could see. But we never told Brother Justin that.

Brother Justin had many clever tricks he used to catch us doing evil. He had these thick glasses and he could see backwards out of the inside of them because the reflection allowed him to see back over his shoulder. So if he were writing on the board and one of the barbarians threw a spitball—bam! Brother Justin had caught that barbarian in his web. Then he'd make the miscreant write the Declaration of Independence several times. "The world's greatest document other than the New Testament," he would always say as he gave you this "penance."

But being barbarians we always looked for ways to torture him right back. Jake "the Snake" Jacobsen created the "Vee" game where you pursed your lips, with tongue against your inner, now protruding lip; put your hands behind your head and kept chanting, "Vee! Vee! Vee! Vee! Vee!" When Brother Justin would try to look out of the inside of his glasses to catch who was chanting the "Vee! Vee!" we'd stop abruptly. "Vee! Vee! Vee! Vee!" stop. "Listen you little barbarians," he'd croak. "I'm going to trick you and catch you and then you will have to *memorize* the Declaration!"

In this one area we outsmarted him. We were "Vee" champs. But in other areas he caught us left and right. "Caught you, you little barbarian!" he'd scream when he nailed one of us for some infraction. That cunning old codger would stand outside the classroom but he could look at the reflection of the class in the door's glass window and then he'd come leaping into the room (actually, not leaping, but rather staggering) screaming, "Ah, ha! I tested you and you failed!"

He won the battle of nerves, what education actually is between students and teachers. He piled on massive amounts of homework too. Many a late night was spent doing his "I am reminding you of what you learned you barbarian" work, as he called it.

So one day he was writing something on the board and taking peeks out of the inside of his glasses when he dropped to the floor with a loud thump! Man, this guy would do anything to catch us. The class was silent. Brother Justin's face was to the front wall and his glasses were off.

Jake "the Snake" Jacobsen turned and mouthed to the class, "He can't see us!" And we all put our hands behind our heads and chanted, "Vee! Vee! Vee! Vee! Vee! Vee! Vee! Vee!" The whole class chanted, even top students like Arman Carmen Buddy Frasca the Third and our top, top gun, Hugo Twaddle. "Vee! Vee! Vee! Vee! Vee!"

And then, as so often happens when you are having ecstatic fun as a kid, an adult screws it up, because the principal of the school, Brother Augustine, came strolling by just then, and looked in the class. He had heard our thunderous veeing from down the hall. He saw Brother Justin sprawled on the floor and looked up at our class, which had stopped "veeing" as soon as we saw Brother Augustine.

Brother Augustine went over to the fallen Brother Justin, felt his neck and went to the intercom. "Bring a stretcher and call an ambulance. Brother Justin has . . ." He looked over the class of young barbarians many of whose eyes were bugged out in fear and wonder. "Brother Justin will need help. Right away."

The nurse came down and so did several other brothers and they gently lifted Brother Justin onto the stretcher. "Don't cover him yet," whispered Brother Augustine. "Do it down the hall."

Brother Augustine escorted the stretcher out of the room. When no adult came back right away, Jake "the Snake" Jacobsen turned to the rest of us, "Do you think he's dead?"

"Naw," said Stephan Godowsky. "He's testing us. Talk and you'll be writing the Declaration fifty times."

So we stayed silent until Brother Augustine finally returned. It seemed like ages since he had left the room. I never saw our class this quiet in all my life. Augustine was pale-faced and very upset but I could see he was making an effort to calm himself.

"Young men," he started. Young men? We were nowhere near being young men. We were boys, kids, barbarians, but young men? That wasn't us.

"Young men," said Brother Augustine, now completely calm. "Brother Justin has passed on to his eternal reward in Heaven." Heaven? Come on, I thought, this guy was roasting in Purgatory where he would suffer a long time for torturing all of us. "He died in his classroom as he always lived as a teacher of young men such as you. He was a great Brother, a great friend to all of us, a man to be admired." Admired? For what? Being able to look in back of him from the inside of his glasses? "He loved his students."

Oh sure, and I can fly.

"I know this comes as a shock to all of you," said Brother Augustine. "When you are young you never think of death being near to you. But as the Holy Catholic Church teaches, God can take us at any time and that time only He knows. That is why we must always go to confession, receive Holy Communion and be good so we go to our reward in Heaven where we will see God face to face and not be sent to Hell where the souls of the tormented sinners go like Hitler and President Roosevelt."

I wondered if maybe Justin had wound up in Hell. Would God send one of His own "brothers" to Hell, even if the brother were creepy? I doubted it. Justin was in Purgatory which is where, we were taught, all of us go after we die to be purged of our sins, except for the Virgin Mary who never had a sin on her soul being the mother of Jesus.

"We have called our main office and we shall have a substitute teacher in here by Monday. All of you please fall to your knees now and we shall pray for the soul of our beloved Brother Justin that it find rest in the arms of God."

We barbarians were all looking at each other. Who the heck wanted to get on his knees for Brother Justin? But we had no choice in the matter, so we slowly got up from our desks and knelt on the hard floor.

"Let us pray," said Brother Augustine. So we prayed, kneeling on the hard floor. We prayed the "Our Father" prayer, then a bunch of "Hail Marys," then the "Nicene Creed," then Brother Augustine asked us if we had any individual things to say. We all looked at each other.

"Some of you might want to say something about our dear Brother Justin," said Brother Augustine.

Then Peter Kendrick, one of the smart kids, raised his hand.

"Yes, young man," said Brother Augustine smiling warmly.

"Do we have to do the homework?"

7

Halloween

Bless me father for I have sinned. I stole water balloons.

As a kid I loved Halloween and I had great times filling up socks with chalk dust in order to whack my friends all over their hair, heads and bodies; and especially those girls who would scream bloody murder if they got even a little bit of chalk dust on themselves.

What fun!

Shaving cream was fun too. Just spread it all over everybody.

Obviously cans of shaving cream had to be stolen from your father's personal stash and many of us just couldn't get our hands on some, or we were afraid to, because fathers in that time and place were not too hesitant to belt their kids should those kids run afoul. Stealing from a parent merited a beating.

In my neighborhood the local supermarkets and family stores wouldn't sell kids those shaving foam dispensers because they knew that we weren't yet old enough to shave, being somewhere around 11 years of age. (This did not relate to Mary Louise Roncallo, of course, who could have starting shaving at birth.)

I never threw eggs because my mother said, "Frankie, you can blind someone if you accidentally hit them in the face, so no eggs." So it was no eggs.

But the ultimate in fun times were the water balloons. Four of us (we called ourselves The Four Horsemen) used to go up to the roof of the Flagg Court apartment building right across the street from the public library in order to bomb library patrons who crossed the street and got within range of our water bombs.

Flagg Court was a really tall apartment building, actually an apartment complex of several buildings, and we had a unique way of getting onto the roof, which the superintendent of the building knew nothing about. We knew how to unlock the roof door from the inside even without the key. Mike Munch discovered that secret; he was a really clever kid; really street smart. And to keep our secret a *top* secret, we only did this on Halloween evening when it got dark. We figured we'd be able to do this until we were old men of thirty. Water ballooning was the absolute best!

So it was the day before Halloween and Munch said to us, "Oh, I got the best balloons. We don't even have to buy them. My father has them in the drawer of his night table."

"Why would your father have balloons?" asked Ladislav Hamlin.

"He has a few boxes of them," said Munch.

"Why?" asked Ladislav.

"Maybe he likes to water balloon too," I said. It was logical, wasn't it? If you had some boxes of balloons in your night table, why else would they be there? Even parents might find water ballooning fun. It didn't have to be restricted to kids. They probably didn't tell us about this because they didn't want to give a bad example as giving "bad example" was a sin.

"Makes sense to me," said Jake "the Snake" Jacobsen.

"Look, these aren't the normal crummy balloons you get at Bedel's Stationary that break before you even get them half filled; these are special," stated Munch definitively.

"How do you know they are so special?" asked Hamlin.

"Each one comes wrapped in its own wrapper. You have to break the wrapper to get the balloon out," said Munch. "I took one and did a test when my parents weren't home. The balloon is so strong it holds a ton of water!"

"Wow," said Hamlin.

"They must cost a lot," said Jacobsen.

"But we are going to get them for free. I think I can take enough of them without my father noticing it," said Munch.

"We don't even have to pay for them," I said. "We can get even more chalk for our socks."

"They have their own name too," said Munch, now really proud of the fact that he had let us onto the greatest water balloons of all time. "They have a horse on the wrapper. It's some Greek name about the horse that destroyed Troy."

"Troy Donahue, the actor?" asked Jacobsen.

"Troy is a city in Rome," said Hamlin confidently.

"A horse destroyed a city?" I asked. "Come on."

"It was a really big horse if you see the wrapper. A really big one," said Munch.

"It's probably like a fairy tale," said Hamlin. "Like Santa. It's for little kids who like stories about horses."

"Well these babies of your father's are gonna be our horses!" laughed Jacobsen.

"Bombs away!" I screamed.

"Down with Troy!" yelled Hamlin.

Halloween night at 5:30 and it was getting dark at this time now. We did the sock and shaving cream thing while it was still light and we had dozens of girls screaming as we chalked them and covered them in foamy soap. Now it was time to climb the stairs to the top of Flagg Court and get those water balloons ready for combat.

Munch had gone home at around five o'clock to get the balloons since his mother usually picked up his sister at her swimming lessons at that time and his father was not yet home from his work. Munch's dad was a cop—a big, scary, mean-looking cop you didn't want to mess with. Munch's mother always said that Mr. Munch, whom she called "Boo-Boo," was a "big teddy bear" but he looked more like a grizzly if you asked me. If I were a criminal I wouldn't want to mess with Mr. Munch.

Mike Munch was already on the roof with a whole box of these special balloons. I read the label and it said these balloons were extra strong and could be relied on not to break. Great! This would be the Halloween night of all nights. Get ready library patrons.

We started opening the wrappers.

"They're all one color," said Jacobsen.

"Doesn't matter," said Hamlin. "They feel really strong." He stretched one of them to loosen it up. "Wow! These things stretch like crazy."

On the roof there was a water spigot and a hose. The spigot was missing the turning knob, which the superintendent had in his sole possession, but Munch had taken care of this problem too. He brought his own knob from his house. Munch was the only kid to live in his own house; the rest of us lived in apartments.

I put water in my balloon first. "Holy Moses!" I said. "God, this thing is filling up like crazy. It's stretching like crazy too. It's gigantic!" I stopped putting water in. "I don't want this balloon to rip and explode water all over me."

"Let's give yours a try and then The Four Horsemen start the big bombardments baby," said Munch.

"Yaaaahhhhhh!" said Jacobsen.

"Yaaaahhhhhh!" said Hamlin.

"Yaaaahhhhhh!" said I.

Now, our usual Halloween balloon bombing had to be executed carefully. You didn't want the victims to know the balloons were coming from the roof. If they did, you had to get the heck off the roof really fast or the victim, hopefully soaking wet, could go to the superintendent, whose apartment was right on Ridge Boulevard, the street where the library was.

There was a big sign on the superintendent's outside door that said "Superintendent." It didn't take much to go up to his door and ring the bell. So we had to be really careful not to give ourselves away. We had to make sure the victim was the only one coming down the street. If someone else came out of the library or was walking along the street, we held off the attack because they could catch sight of the balloon sailing off and coming down from the roof and know we were up there.

At the edge of the roof we waited. I held the biggest water balloon ever created. It undulated in my hands. I actually had to hold this huge monster with both hands. An old lady came out of the library using a walker. I could see she had a cast on her foot. Usually people with a broken foot used crutches but she was using a walker. The lady was also quite fat. Maybe the crutches would break because of her weight and that's why she had to use that walker. Whatever, she was the first intended victim.

"Oh, man," said Hamlin. "She looks like a tank."

"Come on lady, cross the street," said Munch.

And she made her way slowly across the street.

Luckily Ridge Boulevard was not a very busy road. This slow moving tank made her way to the sidewalk on our side.

"Come on, come on," said Munch. "Turn this way tanko and get your punishment."

As she walked towards us, I got the gigantic undulating balloon ready. It was rare that we actually achieved a direct hit on someone's head, although that was the goal, but still a water balloon smashing close by was sufficient to get people wet enough to piss them off and look up and down the street to see what rotten kid threw the damn thing.

"Like aim to drop it down about a foot in front of her so she walks into it. This baby will explode all over her head!" laughed Munch.

"Oh, yeah," laughed Jacobsen.

She was almost under us now. She'd push the walker in front of her, then step forward; walker, step, walker, step, walker, step.

I was timing her.

"Here goes," I said, leaning over the abutment at the edge of the roof. And I let the balloon go. It looked like a giant anaconda snake as it made its way through the air, heading for the large woman.

"I think you got her!" yelled Jacobsen as the balloon was almost at her head.

And then two things happened. The superintendent walked out of his apartment just as the super balloon hit her on the neck; full hit; right on the neck.

But the balloon didn't break. Instead it curled around her neck just like a bolo and brought her to the ground. She was crawling on the ground with this super balloon wrapped around her neck and the superintendent ran to her. But he looked up and saw Jake "the Snake" Jacobsen.

"Holy shit," said Jacobsen, ducking down. "I think he saw me."

"I think we might have killed her," said Munch.

I peered over the edge. "No, she's alive, rolling around on the ground moaning. Now the super's wife is helping her up. Jesus, the balloon still isn't broken."

"Where's the super?" asked Hamlin.

"He's on his way up," screamed Jacobsen and The Four Horsemen bolted to the door just as it opened and a winded superintendent stood there glaring balefully at us.

"You little fucking bastards; you almost killed that woman with that Trojan. What the hell's the matter with you?" he yelled. Man, he had some deep voice. His face was puffy and he was sweating. He was scary.

"We didn't mean it," said Hamlin.

"Some kid dared us to do it," lied Jacobsen.

"We didn't want to kill her," I said.

"It was just some fun," said Munch.

The superintendent grabbed the defiant Munch by his collar. "Yeah, kid, well you can tell it to the cops."

"His father is a cop," said Hamlin thinking this would save us. It didn't.

"Good, good," said the superintendent. "I hope he beats your ass."

Needless to say the cops were called. The lady gave her testimony and the unbroken balloon was there as evidence. The cops were laughing when they saw the balloon.

"Oh, man, where did you get this?" asked one cop.

"My father had these balloons in a drawer by the bed," said Munch, now scared that when his father found out about his arrest (we thought we were going to be arrested) Munch would see his last days.

Munch then tried to save himself. "I figure if my father used water balloons, why couldn't I?"

The cops tried to suppress their laughs but failed.

"You're Munch's kid?" asked one of the cops. Munch nodded.

"Oh, this is going to be fun at the station," said the other cop.

"Every man should be allowed to play with some water balloons," laughed the first cop.

"I agree," said Munch, thinking he had saved himself.

"Oh, yes, we agree, too," said the second cop. "I am sure we can discuss this with your father at the station."

The four of us were taken down to the station and our parents were called. They all arrived at about the same time since everyone lived within a few blocks of the precinct station. The parents were mortified. Mr. Jacobsen whacked Jake in the head, yelling: "What the hell is wrong with you throwing those things at people?" He got slapped again, this time in back of the head.

Then Jake tried to forestall any more whacks and pointed to me and said, "Scobe threw it. I was just there to watch." Mr. Jacobsen smacked him on the arm.

"Don't try to lie your way out of this one," said Mr. Jacobsen as he took Jake by the ear and escorted him out of the precinct house.

Hamlin's mother came, was told what her son did, and cried. That was infinitely worse than having your father belt you. I was praying my mother wouldn't come. I'd rather be clobbered by my father than see my mother break down and cry.

"Mom, mom, I didn't do anything," whined Hamlin.

"I am so disappointed in you," cried Mrs. Hamlin as she escorted her head-hanging forlorn son out of the station house.

Munch's father was next in the station house. He looked around the station at the smiling policemen.

"What's going on?" asked Mr. Munch.

"Oh, Officer Munch, your son stole some of the *water balloons* you keep in the drawer by your bed," said the night sergeant.

"Those *Trojan* ones," said another cop.

"Yeah," said a third cop.

A fourth cop held up the water balloon, which still had not broken: "Here's the evidence Officer Munch."

Mr. Munch's face went red. His eyes bulged. I didn't understand why he was getting that upset about some stupid water balloons. He started towards his son.

In an attempt to stop Mr. Munch from decapitating Munch, I said: "Mr. Munch we can pay you back. I'll buy you some balloons tomorrow. Different colors too."

All the cops laughed. Mr. Munch's face got even redder. His head looked as if it were pulsating.

"Shut up," he said to me. I shut up and prayed he wouldn't shoot me.

Mr. Munch grabbed his son by the hair and pulled him towards the front door.

"Don't let him take any more of your water balloons," cautioned the fourth cop.

Munch was already crying like a baby. "You won't be able to sit on your ass until you're thirty years old," growled Mr. Munch. The other cops were laughing their heads off now. What was so funny? My friend looked like he was about to have all his hair pulled out by the roots and these cops were laughing like crazy. Munch wouldn't be able to sit on his butt until he was thirty and the cops laughed at this?

Then my parents came in. They were told what I had done. My father looked at me in anger. My mother looked at me in sorrow. I bowed my head, knowing I had disgraced them both over some stupid water balloons and a fat old tank using a walker.

When I got home I got it from my father. He whacked me once in the face; then slapped the hell out of my ass. I was wondering, as I felt the stings of each of my father's whacks, whether my father or Munch's father hit harder. I felt that I might not be able to sit down until I was forty.

None of us ever went water ballooning again.

8

Animal Magnetism

Bless me father for I have sinned.
I wanted an icon that would help me attract girls.

When I was hitting puberty and developing this acute fascination with girls, I had heard some of my mother's friends say that Clark Gable and Marlon Brando had animal magnetism. The women also said that these men were just so unbelievably attractive because of that magnetism. And I thought logically, "Hey, all I need to do to make the girls love me is get some animal magnets and hang them from my neck."

I went to John's Hardware store and asked John himself, "I want to buy some animal magnets."

"Huh?" said John.

"Animal magnets," I said.

"What are those?" asked John.

"Don't you have them?"

"I don't even know what they are. I have magnets of all shapes and sizes but I never heard of animal magnets. Tell me what they are and maybe I have them under some other name."

"Uh, ah, hum, uh, they are, ah, uh, hum . . . ."

"Yes? Yes?" asked John. "Come on, I have inventory to do."

"You know magnets that make girls like you. So you have animal magnetism," I stammered, surely as nervous as I had ever gotten.

"Oh," smiled John, "I'm afraid we all want those but they aren't for sale anywhere any more."

It wasn't until a while later that I realized "animal magnetism" was not caused by outside magnets but by something within an individual.

I wish that I could have found those animal magnets because it was much tougher making women like me using my wit and humor. That took work. It isn't easy to display your intellectual talents in five seconds in order to pick up a girl. My standard line, "Hey, do you like math?" usually bombed.

The magnets would have made my love life so much easier. Just put them on a chain around my neck and let nature do its work.

9

Kissing

Bless me father for I have sinned. I find it hard to control myself.

In seventh grade I lived with a perpetual boner, except when I was playing ball. All I dreamt about were girls. I had no idea of what a girl looked like totally naked—I wouldn't know that until I saw a picture when I was a senior in high school—but I could fantasize. Since the girls and boys did not go to the same building for school, we only saw the girls in their portion of the schoolyard when they came out for recess or for lunch. They always looked so clean and well groomed while most of the boys looked a little sweaty and disheveled because we tended to run around a lot.

The girl I loved the most was Mary Sissallo, which was a pure love, but I loved all the other girls in a boner-producing way. What was it about girls that fascinated me? I wasn't the only one either. Except for weird William Carson, who said he couldn't stand girls, all the boys were hawk-eyed when the girls were within sighting distance.

But all of us also knew that those girls were a serious occasion for mortal sin. Most of us were still practicing a daily "loss of seeds," which was a mortal sin, but some of us were now at the stage where we were thinking about actually kissing girls as well as just fantasizing about them.

We had two major questions in this area:

1. What kind of kissing was a venial sin?
2. What kind of kissing was a mortal sin?

There was nothing actually written about this in our catechism and it was never discussed in your home.

So we asked Brother Jonathan about it. Brother Jonathan was the nicest of all the teachers I ever had at our Lady of Angels and one of the three teachers who had the greatest impact on my life. ("Francis," said Brother Jonathan. "Some day you will be a professional writer.") The other two were Brother Barnabas and Sister Patricia Michael.

"Brother," said Jake "the Snake" Jacobsen, "I have something I want to . . . ah . . ."

"Yes?" said Bother Jonathan.

"It has to do with kissing," said Steven Gardell as Jacobsen found himself at a loss for words.

"Kissing *girls*," added Stephen Godowsky, looking at weird William Carson.

"What about it?" asked Brother Jonathan.

"When is it a sin?" I asked. "Or is it always a sin?"

"We're not talking tongues," said Eugene O'Toole.

"Tongues?" I asked. "What does that mean?"

"You stick your tongue in her mouth and rub them together," said O'Toole.

"Okay, okay," smiled Brother Jonathan. "Let's go easy here." Then he thought a moment. "Tongues are always a mortal sin until you, ah, until you go to college or are over eighteen." I had no idea at that time that Brother Jonathan was kind of making up some of the rules since there were no hard and fast rules in this area of Catholic theology. According to some of the girls, the nuns of Our Lady of Angels were much stricter. No kissing was allowed except if you were engaged and then only a little peck on the lips. I'm glad I didn't have the nuns—almost everything with them was a sin.

"How long if you are kissing regularly, no tongue," said Arman Carmen Buddy Frasca the Third, "before you fall into the mortal sin range?"

"What are you thinking of when you are kissing?" asked Brother Jonathan.

"I don't know," said Arman.

"Say, uh, you are thinking thoughts that could lead to self abuse?" asked Jake "the Snake" Jacobsen.

Brother Jonathan smiled. "Well, you have to try not to think those thoughts." He saw our faces. "I know, I know, that is very hard, but what you think is often how God judges what is or is not sinful."

"Say I am saying a prayer when I kiss," asked Hugo Twaddle. "How long can I go before I commit a mortal sin?"

Brother Jonathan laughed, "I never heard of anyone praying in that situation . . . actual prayer praying."

"Say I have like nothing on my mind?" said Valentine Zumwalt. "Can I keep kissing for hours?"

"Okay," said Brother Jonathan. "Let me see if we can get a framework around this issue. Just a friendly kiss between a girl and a boy is not a sin. If you like the girl and the girl likes you a friendly *little* kiss would be okay in the eyes of God. Now, too many boys get too aggressive and start to want a lot more than just a friendly little kiss. They want to really—well, you understand, right?"

Since every boy in the class had been living with a giant boner every day, we all understood what he meant.

"Prolonged kissing, one that really affects you physically and makes your mind a little, how do I put this? It makes your mind a little crazy, that is a venial sin. Tongues or pressing up against her too much and too hard could be considered a mortal sin if you do this while you are kissing."

"What about dancing?" asked Steven Gardell.

"Pressing hard while dancing?" added Arman.

"It's called grinding," said Eugene O'Toole and we knew then that O'Toole had probably been the farthest with the girls. He was a big, strong, muscle-bound kid who looked a lot older than a seventh grader. I'm guessing he had even touched the girls' blossoming breasts—which part of a girl's anatomy all the boys had become fixated on.

In fact, not a day went by than one of us commented on the breasts of this or that girl. This was a time when the breasts of the girls were really growing and showing.

"Did you see Laura Don?" said James Gallagher. "God, her boobs are really getting big." Laura Don was the knockout of Our Lady of Angels among the seventh grade girls. There was many a boner-laden dream about her among all of us—probably every evening.

"If you are looking for true guidance," said Brother Jonathan thoughtfully. "You should look inside yourselves and perhaps ask yourself that if this girl you are with were your mother or sister what would you do with them then?"

"I'd puke," said Steven Gardell.

"I don't have a sister," said Valentine Zumwalt.

"I don't mean it literally," said Brother Jonathan. "If someone, if the girl . . . okay, how's this? Treat all girls the way you would want your mother or your sister to be treated."

In the schoolyard the next day, we were discussing the sinfulness of prolonged kissing and "grinding" while we danced.

"You know," said Jake "the Snake" Jacobsen. "You can do the kissing and grinding on Friday night so you only have to get to confession on Saturday. That's maybe sixteen hours. You can confess that, you know, ah, along with."

"Yeah, yeah, okay," said Stephen Godowsky.

"Keep the sins bunched up at the end of the week is the best," said James Gallagher. "THE BUS only has about half a day to kill you then."

10

My Sister Sue

Bless me father for I have sinned. I taught my sister how to fight.

My sister Susan, born on September 16 in 1953, and six years younger than I, was decidedly different; a kid who didn't follow the trends and molds of the girls of the 1950s or early 1960s . . . in fact, she doesn't follow the trends today either.

From ages five through nine she always pretended to be a cowgirl, preferring to play with toy guns from her double-gun holster and wearing her cowgirl clothes and her big cowgirl hat just about every day. She was indeed quick on the draw, having practiced endlessly, and she also had a little boy friend, Tommy, who loved her. Tommy was a gentle kid, the total opposite of my sister, and he followed her around as if he were her puppy. Susan bossed him around as if he were her puppy too. Tommy was her Rin Tin Tin.

Susan actually did have a puppy for awhile. While I had a cat that lived about two years in the family before my mother gave it to the "cat-lady," a ratty old battle-axe who had millions of mangy cats in her apartment before she was arrested for animal cruelty, Susan had always wanted a dog "just like Rin Tin Tin," the military dog that helped to settle the wild, wild west by alerting the noble blue-uniformed soldiers to the advance of the savage scalp cutting Indians all of whom looked in the movies as if they were Italians.

Unfortunately, Susan's puppy only lasted two weeks. If you viewed Susan as different, well that puppy of hers was downright weird, as in *really* weird, as in *totally* insane, as in this thing couldn't walk forwards—it could only walk *sideways*. It had no sense of direction, always hitting its middle into the parking meter poles and not being able to go any further since it was equally balanced between its rear end and its head. So it just kept pressing against the metal pole, going nowhere and bending in the middle even more. You'd have to come and push it to one side or the other for it to continue walking sideways down the avenue.

People always gave you strange looks when they saw you walking that creature. Who could blame them? The beast was always growling—at nothing. It's not as if it focused on you and growled or barked; the way a normal dog does. No, Cleo (that was its name) just growled as if it saw what wasn't there or maybe saw something that was there but no one else could see it. Other dogs avoided her, walking as far away as their owners' leashes allowed. You know that is weird since dogs usually take their meetings on the streets as appropriate times to smell each other's rectums.

Cleo ate anything that came near her mouth, including parts of her own body, or your body, or the body of anyone on the street that walked past. Cleo's face didn't look right. It was bent in one direction and the top of its head was a little twisted, as if someone had been turning a headlock on her in the womb.

Cleo also pooped like a maniac; spewing stinking brown and yellow liquid stuff in all directions. Cleo's poop could explode out of her going five feet into the air. Cleo was the poop version of Mary Louise Roncallo.

My mother and father knew within a couple of hours that this beast had to go, but they felt they had to explain to Susan why they were going to bring Cleo back to the pound where, we all knew, Cleo would be gassed to death.

Susan didn't want to hear it. Heck, she was just a little kid even with her big cowgirl hat and two fake guns with the fake marble handles.

But as the two weeks progressed even a little kid knew something wasn't right with this dog.

"How come she walks sideways?"

"She is always pooh-poohing everywhere."

"She pooh-poohed into my face!"

"She bit herself again. Why does she do that?"

"She ate another dog's pooh-pooh."

"She walks in circles all the time."

So my parents finally brought the dog to the pound where she has now become a hazy, distant memory of the weirdness that life can have in store for its creatures great and small.

Yes, I enjoyed my relationship with my sister. She was fun to torture, which is the job of a big brother after all. And, yes, I did confess this torture every week to the priest but I just kept doing it. The priests were far more concerned about us losing our seeds than about us tormenting and traumatizing our little sisters.

I loved Susan's nose—it was actually the perfect nose and had plastic surgery of pampered teenage girls been popular way back then, all the girls from Long Island and the other rich suburbs would have clamored, "Daddy, daddy I want *that* nose, the Susan Nose."

To confess: I enjoyed putting spit on her nose.

I didn't actually "thwark" phlegm onto her nose, my "thwarking" aim wasn't that good and I didn't want to get it all over her face either. I mean I did love her. I would just put the spit on my finger and touch the tip of her nose and say, "Gotcha!" She would then go ballistic, which was fun to watch, and then she'd start swinging at me whereupon I would hold my arm out and put my hand on her forehead and she couldn't reach me with her flailing punches.

I used to put a sheet on the clothesline out back, the tops wrapped around some newspapers for a head. We lived above a store in those days and the clothesline went from our apartment to a wooden pole in the backyard of the store below us. I made the sheet have a ghostly face and then I would yell out, "Susan! There's a ghost in the back yard!"

Being curious she'd run to the living room window, which overlooked the back yard, and she'd see this thing bouncing and going back and forth in the backyard. Of course, I was in the kitchen doing this special effects work with the clothesline.

Susan would jettison like a bullet back into her bedroom and hide under the covers. I'd come in a few minutes later.

"Is it still out there?" she said shivering from under the covers.

"No, no, I took out a cross and it flew away."

"I hate those ghosts," she said, her head coming out from under the covers. "Why do they keep coming around?"

"I think they like you," I said.

"I hate them."

"I'll protect you. I'm not afraid of them."

The best joke I ever played on her got me a beating from my father and an all-out screaming from my mother. But the pain and temporary deafness were worth it.

Sometimes at dinner I would, when my parents weren't watching, throw food at her. She would throw food back at me too—but she had no subtlety at all and was almost always caught. She'd rat on me in a second, "Frankie threw food at me first!" I'd roll my eyes and scornfully say, "Susan, you can't even lie right." Then I'd look at my mother and father and shrug my shoulders, "Am I going to throw food at a little kid?" My parents bought that for a long time, until the night in question, which made them rethink all their prior assumptions about their Frankie bombarding his sister Susan at dinner.

One night I decided to take the nose thing one step further. I got a couple of peas from the refrigerator and snuck into her room in the middle of the night. There she was, sleeping peacefully, holding her two-gun holster; she was really cute and so was her nose, totally exposed and waiting for my finest achievement.

I leaned down over her, stuck a pea in each nostril, squeezed and ran out of the room. Susan woke up blowing the green stuff out of her nostrils into her hands and I ran back into the room. Her eyes were bugged out and she was holding her hands out so I could see the green stuff.

"Oh, my God, Susan you blew your brains out!" I whisper-screamed, not loud enough for my parents to hear.

"Your brains are in your hands!" I whisper-screamed again. "You might die!"

Then the unexpected happened. Instead of allowing me to take care of the green-brains-in-the-hand problem, Susan leaped out of bed and ran into my parents' room.

"Mommy! Daddy! I blew my brains out! I blew my brains out!"

My mother and father woke up groggy from sleep.

"Huh?" asked my father.

"What?" asked my mother.

"I blew my brains out!" said Susan holding out her hands with the squished green peas. "Frankie said I blew my brains out! Am I gonna die?"

My father looked into my sister's hand. He knew it wasn't brains there. He took some onto his finger, as my mother was doing the same. Peas do have a distinct smell.

"Peas," said my mother.

"Peas," said my father.

"Frankie!" they yelled in unison.

My mother and father both leaped out of bed.

"Are these my brains?" asked Susan.

"They're peas!" said my father.

"Peas?" asked Susan.

"Frankie!" yelled my mother.

"Am I gonna die?" asked Susan.

"Go blow your nose some more," said my mother. "Your nose is dripping peas, don't worry."

Susan ran to the bathroom where I could hear her taking mighty blows of her cute little pea-dripping nose. I thought about running into my room and hiding under the bed but I knew it would be futile. I was in for it.

And I got it too.

Before she was nine I taught Susan how to fight. By this time I was in my teens and I wasn't teasing her much any more. But she wanted to be able to fight like the cowboys on television. So I showed her the Rocky Marciano short right-hand punch that had come in so handy against Ferguson. We'd have little sparing matches which were basically her trying to hit me. She was actually pretty good for a little kid.

One day during a ferocious blizzard, Susan and I were walking home along 3RD Avenue. Susan was dressed in a snowsuit with her cowgirl's hat on top of her hood. She was able to keep it there because she had the strings on it tied under her chin. Even so she had to hold onto it during gusts of wind.

As we came to the mailbox where I had tried to mail Ferguson's head, Susan's hat blew off and I went running after it. That wasn't too easy because the snow had to be around a foot deep. But I got the hat and turned to go back to Susan and there was this kid standing right in front of her. He was pretty big too; maybe fourth grade. Susan was probably in third grade.

He pushed Susan to the ground and then made a big snowball and threw it right in her face—really hard. Then he scooped up snow and poured it on her face. I could hear Susan crying.

I started to run towards them, "Hey! You little fuck!" I screamed. He looked up as he was about to shovel more snow in my sister's face, saw me, and ran across 3RD Avenue, down 71st Street toward Ridge Boulevard which ran parallel to 3RD Avenue.

I lifted Susan up, "Are you okay?"

"Yes," she said and indicated she wanted her cowgirl hat. I put it on her head. I wiped the snow off her face—wiping her tears away too.

"Stay right here," I said. "I'm going after him," and I ran across 3RD Avenue and down 71st street. Going in this direction, I was heading closer to the Narrows Bay. The little shithead was about a half block in front of me but he couldn't run as fast in the snow as I could since I was a teenager and he was a little creepy punk.

I caught him just as he was running across Ridge Boulevard. I dived on him and brought him down in the snow. Now, even at that moment, I knew I couldn't beat the shit out of him. I was probably five years older than he—so I grabbed him by his hood, lifted him out of the snow, grabbed the back of his coat and started to push him back to 3RD Avenue.

He was scared and didn't say a word.

At 3RD Avenue there was Susan in her cowgirl hat, waiting in a doorway of a store, just as I had told her to.

I half dragged the kid across the avenue to Susan.

I stood him straight in front of her.

"You got anything to say?" I asked.

I was expecting an apology but this was Brooklyn and this was a Brooklyn kid who had just figured I didn't intend to beat him to a pulp.

"You got anything to say?" I said again.

"Yeah, fuck you!" he said.

There was a slight pause and then Susan stepped in and threw a perfect right hand into this kid's sneering face. When I say it was a perfect punch I mean it. This stupid kid went down in the snow; his nose bleeding profusely. Now he started crying.

"I didn't mean it; I didn't mean it!" he cried, blood now being absorbed by the snow.

Right, he didn't mean it. He was possessed by the devil maybe? He had pushed my sister into the snow; had hit her in the face with a snowball and then tried to bury her face with snow. Yeah, he didn't mean it. How did it all happen then?

"I should let her kick the shit out of you," I said. Then I took Susan by the elbow and we walked home. Neither of us turned around to look at the kid. He was now a dead issue due to a beautiful right hand delivered by my little sister Susan in her cowgirl hat.

But little sisters do grow up. At 12 years of age, Susan had relinquished her idea of being Annie Oakley in the Wild West and instead had become a little lady, still followed around by the sorrowful Tommy who knew he didn't have a chance in the love department.

Then Susan got her period.

My mother took her aside and explained to her what the period meant and that she was now a woman and could get pregnant if she fooled around with boys. My mother evidently didn't explain this quite right because as I walked home from the Brooklyn-Staten Island ferry, I saw Susan coming towards me, about a block away.

I waved to her; she saw me, and walked across the street. As we passed on either side of the street, I called to Susan, "What are you doing over there?"

"Nothing," she said and walked even faster.

I thought that maybe something was bothering her and she wanted to be alone with her thoughts—whatever kinds of thoughts a 12-year old girl would have.

Something really bothered Susan on this first day of her period. Of course, I didn't know it was the first day of her period since in those days people didn't really speak of these things.

That night, as was his custom, my father went into Susan's room to kiss her good night. Susan threw the covers over her head.

"Susan, Susan," said my father. "What is it? Come out from under those covers. I want to kiss you good night."

Susan's head peered out from under the covers. My father bent over to give her a kiss on the check and Susan shot her hand out, "No, Dad," she said terrified. "Things can happen."

It took awhile to explain to her that just being in the presence of men couldn't make her pregnant. But when my mother told her about sexual intercourse, she turned white. "Nobody is doing *that* to me!" she declared.

Susan now has two beautiful grown up children, Melanie and Jason, and a grandson and is married Tony. Yes, even Susan became an adult. She hasn't worn that cowgirl hat in decades . . . unless Tony knows something I don't.

11

Do Pets Have Souls?

Bless me father for I have sinned. I am a cannibal.

My grandmother Rose, my mother's mother, came from the old country, Italy. She had six kids—Mary, Theresa, my mother, Steve, Madeline and Annie.

Nana Rose lived on 92nd Street in Bay Ridge—her house taken by public domain in order to build the Verrazano-Narrows Bridge. Her house was where the 92nd Street entrance ramp is today.

Three of her daughters and their husbands lived in apartments in the building. You entered the building and on the right was Aunt Mary and Uncle Nick's apartment. At the end of the hall was Aunt Annie and Uncle Rocco's apartment. Both Uncle Nick and Uncle Rocco had big fish tanks.

Upstairs there were two apartments. The right hand one was my Aunt Tess (Theresa) and my Uncle Phil's apartment; the left hand one was my Great (big) Aunt Mary and my (skinny) Great Uncle Jim's apartment.

Great Aunt Mary was a massively large, balding, mustachioed woman who gave birth to her son in the toilet bowl. "Gee, I think I have to go to the bathroom," she said one night to Great Uncle Jim, who snored away.

Great Aunt Mary had no idea that she had been pregnant.

"Jim, Jim," she whispered into her husband's ear. "You now have a new son."

"Good," said Great Uncle Jim turning over and snoring again.

Appropriately, this son became a sanitation worker.

One Easter I received a half dozen baby chicks as a present. In those days children could not only get baby chicks but baby turtles and baby alligators and piranhas as pets. It was a looser time in American history. At some point or other I had all of those other creatures as pets. Sadly, they all died before their time—which meant none of them were really geared to the living arrangements I gave them in New York City. The turtles got soft shells and passed on in their little "turtle bowls" that looked like a plastic track with an island and a fake tree in the middle. The alligators wouldn't eat the bananas I fed them and they died in a month. I couldn't understand why these creatures wouldn't eat bananas since the chimps in Tarzan movies only ate bananas and they came from Africa too. The piranha was a lonely thing in a tiny fish tank. It died within three days.

Since I had to distinguish each chick from every other chick my mother put different colored ink on each one's tail feathers. Four of them quickly met their demise but two, Floe and Joe, thrived.

On Sundays we all gathered in Nana Rose's basement. All the relatives from all over Bay Ridge would have their Sunday dinner there—we ate from noon to night. All the cousins were there. The cousins had fun playing and putting on shows for the adults.

Nana Rose was from the old school, not just the old country. One Sunday Nana Rose said, "Frankie (she pronounced it Frang-gay) we gonna eat chickens today."

I couldn't handle that and begged that she not break the necks of Floe and Joe. That's how she would do it—grab them by the necks and twist until they died. I screamed "What if they had mortal sins on their souls?" since I had seen them pecking at each other's beaks and one occasionally mounting the other. I knew the beak-pecking was a form of kissing and outlawed by the Church. I loved my chickens even though they had committed mortal sins. I didn't want to see their souls roasting in Hell after we had roasted them in the oven.

And an even bigger question loomed large in my head. Would eating a bird that was in a state of mortal sin cause you to ingest their sinfulness? Could I go to Hell by such an act? After all, when you ate Christ didn't he enter your soul? Why would it be different with chickens?

But Nana Rose was adamant. My mother explained that birds had no souls and therefore could not sin. I was skeptical of my mother's advice ever since I discovered she had lied to me about Santa Claus. If a person could lie about such a big thing as Santa Claus how could I trust her about chickens? So I stood my ground.

I went to my aunts who all agreed with my mother. I just assumed they did so because they were all sisters.

Then I went to the men. I thought they had the power in the family and their word would be law. I had no idea that they had absolutely no power in the family since they were all married. Anyway, they laughed at my predicament and explained that was the fate of chickens—they were born to be eaten. My Uncle Steve, the hunter and war hero, disdainfully said he had probably killed thousands of chickens. "I'd eat them raw if I was hungry enough. Grow up and shut up."

Uncle Steve was gruff. He used to twist my arm until I cried and try to get me to say, "My father is a bum." I wouldn't say it but I cried and cried until he let me go saying, "You're a little baby Frankie. Grow up." The other uncles never did anything mean. The aunts never stopped Steve. I had no idea that since he was the only boy in an Italian family he was the golden child despite his ways.

So not a one of them—no aunts, no uncles, nor my mother, nor my father—lifted a finger to save Floe and Jo. To them it was just the natural course of things.

I refused to eat Floe and Jo—at least at the start of the meal. But eventually my little-boy hunger won out and I blessed myself and devoured pieces of my two pets. I was sad I did it but hunger makes killers of us all.

Since they had been defeathered I took the feathers and buried them in the backyard. I said a prayer and then went inside for dessert.

Prior to 1998, the distinct order of power in my house went this way: My wife the Beautiful A.P. ruled; I followed, then the boys Greg and Mike trailed the pack—in short, a normal marriage.

Then a very nice teacher named Alicia Dunn (whom I shall never forgive) brought us a wonderful, little green bird, known as a Quaker Parrot, and we adopted it. The bird was a baby and we fed it with a feeding syringe. We named it Augustus because Quaker Parrots are also known as "The Little Emperors" and Caesar Augustus was arguably the greatest of the Roman Emperors.

The Quaker Parrot is called a Quaker Parrot because it quakes—it shivers and its head goes up and down. Needless to say it is pretty weird looking the first time you see it.

However, Augustus hasn't quaked once in the 15 years we've had him. He is the un-quaked Quaker Parrot in our house.

But he *is* the emperor.

The new order of power in the Scoblete household is now this:

1. Augustus
2. A.P.
3. All other people, places and things on earth
4. Me

I thought Augustus should be on the bottom, exactly where my pet chickens were when I was a kid. Nana Rose had it right.

I tolerate Augustus—actually he tolerates me; but we get along okay. Still, the true love of his imperial life is my beautiful wife A.P. Augustus loves her with his whole heart and beak. He kisses her, making a smacking sound which now I know is not a mortal sin; he grooms her; rubs his head against her; sits on her lap when she reads. He eats breakfast with her. He calls for her when she leaves him in a room alone. Being a flock creature, Augustus wants to be with the flock, that's A.P. and me. Given the choice between the two of us, Augustus will always prefer A.P. Well, I prefer A.P. over Augustus.

Many people think that parrots don't change their expressions, that their faces always stay the same. This is absolutely not true as anyone who owns a parrot can tell you.

While the parrot *seems* to be unable to change the expression on his face, when you see a parrot kissing, being kissed, grooming your wife or yourself, or showing signs of distress or anger, that face *is* different—even though a photo would show it looking the same as always . . . so much for science.

Augustus revels in A.P.'s attentions and his face shows it without changing outward expression—Augustus exudes emotion like some psychic force. When A.P. and I have been away on a trip for several days—Augustus is clearly displeased and lets her know it. While he likes his babysitter, she is not his mistress, merely his temporary caretaker. A.P. is the woman in his life. A.P. is the love of his life. Yes, it is kind of creepy.

Of course, to a parrot a woman has to know her place in life too—and that place is beneath him.

For A.P. to get back into Augustus' good graces after a trip, she must grovel non-stop for many hours, subjugating herself to his emotional mastery, which A.P. happily does. She has never—not a single time in our decades of marriage—groveled for me.

"Oh, I'm sorry, I'm so sorry," croons A.P. while Augustus ignores her. "Oh, I left you and I am so sorry that I left my good little bird. I love my good little bird [she kisses Augustus making that smacking sound] and I want him to love me again. That's a good little bird. Oh, I am so sorry I left you [kiss, kiss]." Yes, kind of creepy.

Augustus allows this for a good half day, A.P. begging forgiveness, before he starts warming up again and cuddling and returning her kisses.

I don't do the begging routine. Augustus knows I don't care if he likes me or not—although he tolerates me and does not get antagonistic as some parrots do with the spouses of their main loves. Parrot bonding behavior can be tough on the un-bonded spouse but I don't have those worries, thankfully. Augustus and I co-exist.

Now bird scientists go bonkers when we bird owners ascribe human emotions and characteristics to our feathery flock mates but I have no doubt that Augustus is one smart little creature. Yes, scientists can froth at the mouth all they wish when I write this but Augustus knows exactly what he is doing when we spend our days together. He *thinks*. He has a brain—albeit a bird brain.

The Beautiful A.P. is a full-time librarian so she is frequently out of the house working; leaving Augustus with me. Since

I spend my entire day writing, Augustus and I share the same tree—meaning my office. I keep Augustus' cage open most of the time, except when he is torturing me with his "fun" games which include:

1. flying into the kitchen to throw silverware on the floor from the drain board

2. flying into the living room to crap on our new couch or on our new chair or on A.P.'s handmade quilts or on my giant HD television set

3. flying onto my shoulder where he immediately dumps a load on me

4. sitting on my shoulder contentedly, grooming the hairs in my ear, until he sees I am not aware anymore of his presence and then biting my ear lobe to let me know he is there

5. flying to me and then deciding not to land but to create a great wind to blow over the papers that are sitting on my desk, sending the papers flying all over the place

6. flying onto the dining room table and shredding the napkins we keep in a basket

Now the reason I know these are deliberate behaviors and not some reflex action has to do with the fact that he will repeat one of these over and over, since I have to get up and get him and bring him back to our tree. If today is going to be the drain board day—he will do it over and over, even after I've taken all the knives, forks and spoons away.

So the game in his clever mind is this:

1. I fly to drain board and throw stuff on the floor.

2. King Scobe (that's my name to him—yes, he can actually say it) comes and brings me back to the cage.

3. He puts me back on top of the perch on top of my cage.

4. He goes back to work.

5. I wait, subtly watching him until he is immersed in his work.

6. Then I fly to the drain board and we do this over again—whether or not there are knives, forks or spoons there.

7. If there are no knives, forks or spoons there he still has to leap up to prevent me from pooping on the drain board and dishes.

The next day will be the couch day. Each day has its own little theme. He knows what he is doing. I can see it on his devious little unchangeable face.

Now Augustus does take the occasional nap during the day; his feathers all puffed up around his face. He also goes through a litany of the words and phrases he knows:

1. I love you.

2. I'm a good little bird.

3. Love King Scobe.

4. Love.

5. Bath! Bath! (This is really more of a shriek than a word, but he wants a bath.)

6. Kiss, kiss.

7. Want a drink.

8. Go schleep. (He says this around 4PM when he wants his cage covered so he can go to sleep—he sleeps 12 hours a day—or, at least, he is in the dark 12 hours a day.)

Augustus and I have made accommodations to each other. We have an understanding, a good relationship since we are part of the same flock. Of course, ultimately I am in the inferior position in our relationship since I must—and I mean *must*—react to what he does since he has the ultimate weapon—wet poop that quickly hardens into a rock. A.P. and I have nicknamed him "the Stealth Pooper."

If he is in the mood for one of his games, which can be categorized as "Get King Scobe to Leap Up and Get Me!" then I have to play that game or he'll poop where the game takes him. So unless I am on a real writing deadline, I play—I figure he's enjoying himself. But when the chips are down and I have to get in an article on a close deadline, then I have to lock him in his cage, where he plays with biting things.

And speaking of biting things.

Augustus actually prefers to bite real things, such as computer keys, computer and telephone wires, books, bills, checks, checkbook covers, pens, pencils, jewelry and watches to name a few. Give him a choice between a wonderfully colored expensive toy bought at a high-powered parrot convention or biting your grimy keys, he prefers the keys. A drab real thing is far more interesting than a colorful toy. He is not unlike my young grandchildren who would rather play with real things than toys. Toys are secondary.

I did once try to get A.P. to get rid of Augustus, using as an excuse that it is a pain in the ass to go away on vacation because she always worries about him. I pulled out a big gun on this one, quoting the "13th Apostle" Paul from Ephesians in the bible: "Wives, submit yourselves to your own husbands as you do to the Lord. For the husband is the head of the wife as Christ is the head of the church, his body, of which he is the Savior. Now as the church submits to Christ, so also wives should submit to their husbands in everything."

I put my bible down and looked at A.P. "You believe this stuff. What do you think about the fact that you must submit to me in everything?"

She laughed, "Paul was single. What did *he* know?"

It was a nice try on my part but fruitless.

Shortly after I tried to *Paulize* the Beautiful A.P. Augustus was put in our wills. He has a long life expectancy and there is a good chance he'll outlive both A.P. and me. Since my sons have said they will deep fry him if we leave Augustus to them, we have decided to give him to a special parrot home—along with a sizeable donation. My fear is that the little guy does have a soul and I'll never get rid of him—in this life or the next.

Right now as I am writing this, Augustus sits on top of his cage planning a trip to the dining room table, where he has flown seven times already. Since I am way ahead of schedule today, I play the game with him. He's nailed me twice with poops so far—one on my shirt and one on my hand. If Augustus were the size of Rodan, the giant bird that destroyed Tokyo in 1956, one poop by him could wipe out an entire city.

I have found in life three sentences that, if followed, will make life a joy. These are:

1. Be honest with yourself.
2. Listen to your wife despite what Paul wrote.
3. Obey your bird.

With those sentences, life can be grand, especially for your wife and your bird. Two out of three ain't bad.

The Apostle Paul was a washout. You know something—where's Nana Rose when you need her?

12

The Real Dream Team

Bless me father for I have sinned. I am guilty of the sin of pride.

When I was in 8th grade at Our Lady of Angels elementary school in Bay Ridge, Brooklyn, our basketball team went undefeated, winning 55 straight games, starting with exhibition games in September (some against freshmen and junior varsity high school teams) and concluding with a big win in an invitational tournament that pitted teams from all over the East. In between, we won our borough, then county championships, and along the way several citywide invitational tournaments composed of the best of the best teams.

At the beginning of the season no one realized just how great our team would be (or as the New York Daily News later called us when we were invited to play in Madison Square Garden: "The powerhouse team that has mowed down all opposition."), although everyone knew we'd be one of the best in the city. In fact, several other teams were rated more highly than we were in the preseason polls (yes, even in 8th grade, New York City teams were closely watched), for example, St. Jude, whose imposing center was a young man standing 6'10" tall named Lew Alcindor (who became Kareem Abdul Jabbar) and the incredible St. Cecilia's of the Bronx which had a win streak of 30 games before we played them.

Our starting team was composed of kids I had played ball with in schoolyards ever since I was a little kid. We were all friends;

schoolmates, though fierce rivals in those schoolyard basketball wars, and teammates at Our Lady of Angels. I can remember them now as if it were yesterday—and as I write this it was over four decades ago!—the real dream team: hard-nosed Stevie Gardell, silky smooth Billy Bell, dogged Douglas Bernhardt, and the awesome 6'8" Patrick Heelan. Our sixth man was leaping Ken Pederson, a 6'3" bundle of energy. Our coach was a brilliant man, Brother Barnabas, of the Franciscan order. He worked us in practice until our tongues would hang out. We worked on pressing the other team; going to the sides for the fast break when Pat Heelan grabbed a rebound; mixing up the defense and offense so we were never predictable.

I was the team leader. It was my job to shut down the best scorer on the other team, a job I relished. Not one hot-shot high-scoring opponent ever scored more than 8 points against me when I covered them because I stuck like crazy glue to them from one end of the court to the other. I was also our second leading scorer, behind the awesome Heelan. And my game "rose to the occasion" when the chips were down.

When we met the undefeated St. Cecilia's in the finals of the St. Francis Prep tournament, they were favored to beat us and their players sneered at us whenever they looked our way. Well, why not, they were 30 and 0, although at the time we were 17 and 0. St. Cecilia's had three guys who could dunk; their backcourt guys were shaving and one of their forwards had a mustache! In their red-silk uniforms, they looked imposing.

In the first three minutes of the game against St. Cecilia's, I stole the ball from their big-shot backcourt six times—in a row! They couldn't even get it past the half court line. We were up 16 to 0 halfway through the first quarter and beat them by 42 points in the game. We had blown out the #2 rated team in the city. The only team considered better than us now was St. Jude.

A month later we faced St. Jude in Manhattan at the LaSalle tournament. We were now the #2 team but the Lew Alcindor led St. Jude was still #1 and they were also undefeated. They were the biggest team we ever faced, with Alcindor at 6'10", and two forwards that were both 6'3." Even their backcourt was big—coming in at 5'10" and 5'9". (Remember we were only in 8th grade.)

This match up between the two best teams in the City drew a SRO crowd to the LaSalle gym. All the newspapers in the City wrote about the battle of the schoolboy giants: Alcindor vs. Heelan, and basketball aficionados came from all five boroughs to see the game.

In the very first quarter Heelan got three fouls and had to sit out the rest of the half. At the time he sat out, the score was tied. When he came back in the third quarter we had a 10-point lead. We got that lead by clawing and fighting and pressing St. Jude until their tongues hung out.

Three of us surrounded Alcindor. We swarmed their backcourt. Ken Pederson even blocked one of Alcindor's shots! I stole the ball out of Alcindor's hand under our basket while he was holding the ball up over his head (it almost touched the rim!). I leaped up, snatched it, and in one motion put it into the basket. We won the game by 15 points, our closest contest of the year. From that point on there was no question as to who was the #1 team in New York City—Our Lady of Angels from Bay Ridge, Brooklyn!

At the end of the season, after our 55th win, I knew, even though I was only an 8th grader, that I had belonged to something special that September through June. We would all go on to different high schools and to other teams and on to life. But no team I ever played with since that season was quite the same.

To be the very best at what you do; to be far and away the very best, is a very, very special feeling, no matter at what age it comes—and when I think of Stevie Gardell, Ken Pederson, Billy Bell, Doug Bernhardt and Pat Heelan I think of them as a picture painted in sacred colors and tinged with gold. I think of our other players too—just as important as our starting six—Joe Gallagher, Beanie Lynch, Joseph Atanasio, Vinny Lynch, Charlie Hasslegren, James Cronin, Louis Dotrina and Bob Murray. We shared something profound that season. We faced challenges together and came through them all. We put ourselves on the line and always put out a full effort. We never beat ourselves, even when going up against intimidating opponents. We faced each team and went at them with all the energy and drive that Brother Barnabas had hammered into us. And we prevailed because we were connected. It was like we were one gestalt organism on that court, even though we were distinct personalities off it.

Sadly, I've lost complete track of all of my fellow teammates. I have no idea how life treated them or how they played the game of life. I moved out of the neighborhood to go to college in 1965 and I never went back.

At this stage of their lives most, if not all of them, would be retired or finishing out the "end run." What will life's judgment be on them? Were they good men?

But I know that for me that one season has colored my entire life. I think in some very real way I have tried to recapture in my adult life some of the sense I had about things during that one year. I acted on stage for 10 years, and produced and directed plays as well. While acting had some of the excitement of that championship season, it was not the same. Writing is fun, though there is no adrenaline rush of victory to it. You work hard on an article or book and then . . . poof, it's out there and, though you occasionally get some feedback, there's no equivalent in writing to facing one of St. Cecilia's players in a contest of skill and will.

I belonged to the real dream team and that dream team now only exists in my memory.

13

Dr. Karshitz

Bless me father for I have sinned. I committed a sin of "omission."

Brooklyn's St. John's Prep High School in my freshman year—I had a full athletic scholarship and our basketball team finished second in all of New York City. But there was more to St. John's Prep than just sports.

Doctor Karshitz was about five thousand years old, about five-foot tall, and he had this gigantic, puffy, poor swimming but colorful gold fish in a gigantic fish tank in the back of his classroom. He was a biology teacher and that gold fish had been with him for several thousand years as well. In St. John's Prep we had both clergy and lay teachers. Doctor Karshitz was a lay teacher.

A pimply, muscle-bound, nasty-bastard of a kid named Sullivan, with whom I had my most vicious fight (see *The Virgin Kiss*), poured Drano into the tank one morning just before Doctor Karshitz entered the class. This was freshman biology and Doctor Karshitz had taught it ever since the day after Adam ate the apple and was thrown out of the Garden of Eden. God did have extreme punishments in the Old Testament, didn't he? Death was the price all mankind suffered for eating a stinking fruit! But you couldn't argue with God could you? I once brought this up in a religion class, "Why do I have to die because someone thousands of years ago ate a fruit?" And the priest looked at me coldly and said, "You better hope God is busy right now or you might get something you don't want!"

The poisoned gold fish started swimming in a weird way pretty soon after the Drano hit him and then the poor thing turned over and looked like some staggering drunk hitting the sidewalk. You could see his gills working hard as he whirled and twisted in the water.

"Hey, Doctor Kar-shit, your fish looks dead," laughed Sullivan and then his dumb cronies yuck-yucked too. Sullivan was the leader of all the freshmen creeps at St. John's Prep.

"It's Doctor Kar-*shy*-tz you stupid monkey! As in shy!" screamed Doctor Karshitz and then he looked into the tank and his fish was swirling around slowly on its last breath. (Do fish have last breaths?) I hated Sullivan and I ran to the back of the room and grabbed the fish out of the tank. "Fill the sink with water!" I yelled. Little Larry Heyman ran to the sink but before he could get there Sullivan tripped him and Larry went sprawling on the floor to the guffaws of Sullivan and his fellow simians.

I ran the fish to the sink and turned on the cold water to fill it up. By now the fish wasn't moving and its gills had stopped too. I placed the fish in the water and hoped the poor thing would revive. It didn't. It died as Doctor Karshitz looked on in horror.

"Poor little fishy died," snickered Sullivan. Yuck, yuck, yuck, laughed his creepy cohorts. Sullivan and all his friends smelled of smoke all the time. They were fiendish cigarette smokers. I was hoping that God let those jerks smoke so much because he was preparing them for Hell . . . but you never knew exactly what God's motivation was.

Doctor Karshitz was angry now. Actually, he was—to some degree—always angry. But right now he was insane with anger.

"I will find the filthy monkey who did this and destroy you!" screamed Doctor Karshitz. "I will destroy the monkey who did this!"

Doctor Karshitz was totally bald and the veins on his head were now in high relief. His face was bulging.

Sullivan snickered; so did his friends. Sullivan's friends basically mimicked everything Sullivan did from snickering and guffawing to bullying and beating up those who were weaker than they, which was almost everyone.

Doctor Karshitz had a series of sayings he constantly threw out at us, even on his good days:

1. You are monkeys!
2. Your parents are monkeys!
3. Your grandparents are monkeys!
4. I am a teacher!
5. You are hopeless defectives!
6. You are retards! (No PC in those days.)
7. I am a teacher and what are you? Monkeys!

So off he went: "You are monkeys! Your parents are monkeys! Your grandparents are monkeys! I am a teacher! You are hopeless defectives! You are retards! I am a teacher and what are you? Monkeys!"

Sullivan and his tribe smiled and snickered. Doctor Karshitz saw them. "What is so funny, you monkeys?" Then to Sullivan who had a big grin on his puffy, pimply face. "You, pimply monkey!" shouted Doctor Karshitz as Sullivan's face turned blood red. "Hey, pimply monkey, you probably did it!"

Sullivan was now just glaring at Doctor Karshitz. "I am calling your parents, you pimply monkey, because you did it!"

"I didn't do nothing," said Sullivan.

"He didn't do nothing," said one of his friends.

"Shut up, you monkeys!" screamed Doctor Karshitz and he picked up and then threw a big, heavy biology text book at the friend of Sullivan. The book hit the kid squarely in the face, because the kid ducked right into the book, and his nose exploded with blood. "There you stupid monkey; look what you made me do! Go to the nurse, you monkey, and have her give you a banana!"

Sullivan's friend left the room, holding a hanky to his bleeding nose. Sullivan now sat still, glaring at Doctor Karshitz. Had Doctor Karshitz been a student, Sullivan would have attacked and mangled the poor guy. That's a weird thing about bad people and criminals, the good people to them are the villains! The cop that arrests you for a crime is the bad guy. It's always someone else's fault if you get caught doing something wrong.

In the Garden of Eden it was the same thing. Read the section and you'll see. Eve didn't tempt Adam to eat the fruit. She just handed it to him and he ate it. But when God asked Adam what he had done, Adam said that the woman you gave me made me eat it. Adam had no guts to admit he ate the damn thing and that he wasn't tempted by Eve. Then Eve, also not wanting to take responsibility for anything either, blamed the serpent. The only one who kept his big mouth shut was the serpent and look what happened to him. He became a snake.

And that's how Sullivan saw the world, too. He hated everyone; blamed everyone; beat up everyone until the one day I did him in.

Doctor Karshitz did not get into trouble for busting up one of Sullivan's friends. These kids came from rough, tough, though believing families, and the parents supported the school because if they didn't their kids would have to go to public school and going to public school was the same as being excommunicated. It was the ultimate embarrassment to be thrown out of a Catholic school into the public schools. Better to have a broken nose! Better to have a broken head. Actually, come to think of it, those kids did have broken heads.

But Doctor Karshitz did call in Sullivan's parents. I saw them as they walked to the principal's office. Father Thomas was the principal and he was a nice guy with white hair, a big bald spot in the back, and a W.C. Field's nose from drinking a little too much wine at mass and other places.

I was passing the principal's office on the way to the locker rooms to change for basketball practice. I decided to listen.

Sullivan's father looked like an older, bigger version of Sullivan as he went into the office—a bloated, burly, angry man, smelling of smoke and booze. Sullivan's mother, a small, stooped woman, was as ugly as the mummy and just as dry looking. She smelled even more of smoke and booze. No wonder they had produced such a monstrous offspring.

The first minute or so was quiet. I'm guessing the principal was just introducing everyone and laying everything out and then: "You two are stupid monkeys!" came Doctor Karshitz's voice from the office. "You produced a retarded monkey of a son. You should beat that kid until he learns respect for the fishes of the sea! He's a murderer of nature and what are you going to do about it? Unless you are dumber monkeys than I thought you were!"

In today's schools, no teacher could talk like that to parents, or students, or even the fishes of the sea without being seriously reprimanded or fired. But this isn't now; it was then.

Doctor Karshitz continued his rant. Finally it was over and there was silence again. Mr. and Mrs. Sullivan left the principal's office soon after this and both looked defeated. Mrs. Sullivan was crying and the tears dripped down her dry face.

The next day Sullivan came in with a black eye and a lumpy cheek. He was even meaner now and the first kid he banged up was Little Larry Heyman. In class he sat sullenly but in the schoolyard and the playing field he made a point of pushing everyone around. And, of course, his friends did the same thing too.

Doctor Karshitz had blamed Sullivan's parents for Sullivan's actions; Sullivan blamed everyone else. He never confessed to the crime but everyone knew he did it, even his parents.

I sometimes wonder where Sullivan is now, probably in prison or dead. If he's dead, I hope he drowned. I should have told on him. But I was silent.

14

Serving and Waiting

Bless me father for I have sinned. I lied.

As a freshman in college my family hit a bit of a trough and needed some infusions of money. Luckily I had a full academic scholarship but, still, I needed spending money and money for books and now I needed to send money home to Mom and Dad.

Even at an early age I was discovering that life was not easy.

Most of the jobs college students could get were minimum wage affairs and I definitely couldn't make enough doing minimum wage work—I had already tried that at a stationary store for minimum wage. Mostly we got older men looking at pornography, a collection for which this store was unrivalled.

"I'm thinking of becoming a waiter," I said to my roommate Bob Joe. Yes, that was his real name, which he subsequently changed when he became an anchorman for CBS news in Syracuse. They gave him a far more sophisticated name, Bob Kirk. That's television for you.

"At the diner?" he asked. Bob was sitting on his bed, totally nude, which he did sometimes to finish the drying process after a shower. That didn't bother me a bit. My very first roommate, the fabulously wealthy Reginald Thurston—he drove a *new* red Mustang convertible given to him by his parents—woke me up the next morning after our very first day on campus in a rather peculiar way.

I was deep in sleep when I heard a fleshy thumping—whack! whack! whack!—and I groggily opened my eyes. I saw a penis, right in front of my face, maybe two feet away, going up and down, up and down, and slapping Reginald Thurston's abdomen and then his balls as he did his "morning jumping jacks."

"Best exercise in the world," proclaimed Reginald. "Gets your juices flowing so you can confront the day!"

"Do you have to get your juices flowing right in front of my face?" I asked.

"You were sleeping," he said, jumping up and down. Whack! Whack! Whack! Whack!

"I'm not sleeping now," I said.

"Hey, baby, my girlfriends all love Mr. Moto," said Reginald.

"Mr. Moto?"

"Yeah, baby"—whack! whack! whack!—"because the eye of my dick looks Chinese."

"Chinese? Mr. Moto's a Japanese wrestler," I said. Reginald was obviously an idiot.

"Japanese, Chinese, who cares?" he said. Whack! Whack! Whack! Whack!

"Would you take Mr. Moto across the room? Over there," I pointed.

Within a week I asked for and got a new roommate, Bob Joe, and the two of us became great friends. So a little nakedness from Bob was no big deal.

"No, not the diner," I said. "I'm thinking of getting a job at the Delanco Hotel."

"Delanco? That's the most expensive hotel in town. Their restaurant has waiters in tuxedos. Do you own a tux?"

"No," I said.

"How the hell are you going to get the job then?"

"I think those tuxes are like their uniforms and are supplied by the restaurant," I said.

"Have you ever waited tables before?"

"No."

"That could be a problem," he said. "That's a fancy restaurant. They aren't just going to hire a novice."

"There's a notice in the local newspaper today that they are looking for a waiter and a waitress," I said.

"Try for the waitress."

"Read this. It's my resume." I handed him a sheet of paper.

"You . . . wait a minute; you said you never worked as a waiter before and look at all these big time New York City restaurants. You worked at these?"

"No," I said. "Here's what I figured. If I tell them I have no experience they aren't going to hire me. If I give them this resume they might call up some of these restaurants and they won't hire me. But if they have to hire someone quickly they may just look at the resume and hire me without checking. I've got nothing to lose." Other than going to Confession that is. But if I were a good waiter I figure it was only a venial sin.

There was only one glitch to my scheme. When I arrived at the restaurant there were five women and three men waiting for these two jobs. The chef came out to speak to us.

"As you know," he said in Brooklynese, "if you had the intelligence and took the time to call us instead of just showing up, we only hire foreign accented waiters because this gives class to the place. So if you don't have an accent—go away."

Three of the women left and the two men left as well. I thought to myself, *Should I leave?*

The chef looked over at me. "Hey, kid, what's your name?"

This was it. Could I pull this off? What did I have to lose?

"My name eez Francois Sgow-blet-tay," I said in my best French accent.

"You're French?" he asked.

"Oui," I lied.

"You speak French?" he asked.

"Oui," I lied.

"So do I," said the Chef.

A Brooklyn accented chef who speaks French. *My ultimate move now—before he kicks me out on my ass!*

"Ceska tu fay aprell lecole?" I asked. It was the only French phrase I knew. I still don't know how to spell it. It meant, "What are you doing after school?"

"You got me," he laughed. "I don't speak French."

Hooray! Hooray! Hooray!

"I prefer to speak English," I said *accentually.*

"Good," he said, now looking at my resume.

"Oui," I said.

"This is pretty impressive," he gazed at me. "You've had a lot of experience waiting tables for someone so young."

"Oui," I lied. "A man must verk."

"Okay, you and Kelly," he looked over at the Irish woman. "You two have the jobs; report this afternoon at 4:30. We'll fit you with a uniform and you'll begin immediately."

"Exsellantay," I said.

The Delanco Hotel had four hundred rooms, all of them suites, with a gourmet restaurant and a café. I arrived at 4:30 that afternoon and a young man greeted me.

"So what are you?" he asked in a Hungarian accent.

"A wait-tour," I said.

"French?" he asked.

"Oui," I said. This was getting pretty easy.

"Pourrais-tu m'aider s'il te plait," he said in perfect French.

I looked at him. He looked at me.

"I'm not Hungarian either," he said with no accent this time. "No one who works here is from another country. I'm Bill."

"Jesus, man," I said, "I thought I just lost the job. I'm Frank, Francois, Scoblete, uh, Sgow-blet-tay."

"Grow a little mustache, that's what everyone thinks French men have; keep the accent but keep it in check; don't overdo it and you will be fine."

Kelly walked in and said hello in an Irish accent.

"You aren't from the sod are you?" asked Bill.

"You can tell the truth," I said. "I'm not French."

She dropped the accent. "I'm Irish but not from Ireland. I've never been to Ireland in my life. I'm a graduate student in literature."

"Keep the accents but keep them in check," he said to both of us.

Bill fitted us with our uniforms. Mine was a tuxedo with the logo of the Delanco Hotel; hers was a black skirt and a white blouse with the logo on the blouse.

"In a half hour you begin. The other staff will help you if you have any problems," said Bill.

"I have a question," I said. "Does the chef . . ."

"Chef Joseph," said Bill. "Always call him Chef Joseph."

"Does Chef Joseph know we are all phonies?"

"He never says; so always use your accent around him. In fact, use it all the time that you are here. Then you'll never make a mistake."

My first night was the night from Hell. I had no experience waiting tables and I had no idea how to take an order. So I wrote down everything that my first table of four patrons said.

"I'll have the porter house steak with peas and a mashed potato with sour cream and bring some extra butter and chives. I want the steak medium rare but drain away the grease. Also a martini, very dry with olives and if you have the olives with blue cheese that would be great. Make it three olives."

"I'll have the veal Marsala with penne pasta with . . . ."

My first order, which came to four pages, tacked up over the grill in the kitchen, elicited this response from Chef Joseph, "What da fuck is dis!?"

One of the female waitresses ran into the kitchen. She knew it was my "novel" that had made Chef Joseph explode. "Oh, I did that, senor, I had trouble understanding so I wrote down everything but I forgot to hand in the proper check. So sorry, senor, I will get the right one."

The waitress, whose name I have forgotten, gave me a quick lesson in how to take an order. "You never were a waiter before?" I shook my head. "Just do the checks like this and you should be all right," she said.

I did that.

But I had other problems.

When you go to the bar and put drinks on your tray, you have to remember to take the drinks off from the outside first or the tray will fall. You have to make the inside glasses, the ones closest to you, the last ones served.

That's logical.

But when you are a nervous wreck as I was that simple, logical method never entered my mind. My first drink tray I served from the inside out and all the outside drinks spilled on this one elderly lady when my tray flipped over due to the unequal weight.

After I helped wipe her off, I learned my lesson about serving drinks.

One guy ordered spaghetti with meatballs. He was all alone at the table. At least this order would be easy, but I didn't count on the water being on the slick floor just outside the door where you left the kitchen—an area that did not have the expensive carpet on it.

"Woooooeeeee!" I screamed as I went flying backwards, knocking over an upright sand-filled ashtray; the food tray landing on the carpet just before the dining room entrance.

I picked myself up and leapt over to where the spaghetti was slathered all over the carpet and I grabbed handfuls of strands, quickly putting them back on his dish. Then I rushed out, trying to be cool, and placed the plate—as cool as could be—in front of him with a cigarette sticking out of it.

His eyes bulged.

"Oh, oh, excuse me, senor," said the waitress who had saved me with Chef Joseph about a half hour before. "I spilled that, and he thought it was your order; it was mine." And she took the dish away. I could feel the sweat dripping down my arms and forehead. I gave a weak smile to the man.

I ordered more spaghetti and meatballs.

"Hey, Francois, didn't you just get that?" yelled Chef Joseph.

"His wife just came and ordered one," I said.

Chef Joseph nodded. He was sweating profusely as the kitchen was about four thousand degrees.

The last indignity upon me and upon half the restaurant came when I brought in the coffee. We were supposed to pour it at the table and leave the fancy coffee container there in case diners wanted seconds.

I didn't even get to serve firsts.

Some idiot pulled away from the table and my foot caught the leg of his chair and I went sailing head first sliding across a table and letting the coffee come shooting out over half the restaurant. People screamed and when the explosion was over a few said they would sue me and the restaurant for scalding them.

"I am from Long Island," screamed a woman, whose face looked as if people had once stood on either side of her head and pulled her skin out really hard and then glued it to either side of her skull, "I will sue everyone here!" Her mouth looked like the Joker of the *Batman* comics.

Her husband rolled his eyes and said "Shut the fuck up, Sadie!"

So ended my first night of being a waiter.

Yet, I quickly got the hang of it and before you could say, "Grrrhhhuioandjeksuthaywwpdfnsieyooowwwbugnitwit," I was allowed to cook the special meals at table-side. Chef Joseph and I got along but he had a mercurial temperament so it was best to tip toe around him during work hours. I guess it was those endless hours he spent in that supernova of a kitchen.

After a time, I had some patrons who wanted me as their exclusive waiter. One Texan who came in once a week looked very much like Barry Goldwater. He was a late eater, entering the restaurant just before we stopped serving at 10PM. He was a big tipper, giving me 25 percent of the bill.

So one evening all the diners had finished and left. I sat in the back with the other servers when I saw "Mr. Goldwater" come in. I had a mouthful of food but I rushed out to serve him.

"Hi, Francois," he said.

"Bonjour," I said, "what vould you like?" Unfortunately, with my mouth full, on the word "vould" I shot out a giant wad of food—right onto his big, black-rimmed glasses. Being quick on the draw, I took a napkin from the table and quickly rubbed his glasses, which were still on his face, and that smeared the food all over the glass. I even got a hunk on his nose and small tidbits fell onto his white shirt.

He was very nice about it. I still got my 25 percent tip. That taught me, once again, something my mother always said, "Frankie, never talk with food in your mouth."

Sex is great, sometimes, or most times, depending on your partner of course—or never which was more my experience if I must tell the truth. I was never promiscuous—you can read about the full extent of my youthful sexual experiences in *The Virgin Kiss*—and I wasn't quick to pick up on those subtle signals girls sent to boys concerning their willingness to do IT. "Frank, let's have sex!" fell on deaf ears. "Huh, what?" I'd ask.

Since the Delanco was also a hotel, there would be room service orders, complete dinners too. This particular night I had an order of two dry martinis, a bottle of expensive wine, and a full course dinner with dessert.

I put all this on the rolling cart—keeping the hot stuff hot and the cold stuff cold. I knocked on the door.

"Just a minute," said a female voice.

The door opened; the female standing there was totally naked. I guessed she was about 30 years old and in a fast glance I could tell she was in excellent shape.

"Where would you like me to put it?" I asked.

"Oh, you know where to put it," she whispered. The image of the BUS entered my mind.

"I'll put it on the table, if you like," I said.

"On the table is fine; on the bed is fine too."

"I'll put it on the table," I said.

"Do you have a girlfriend?" she asked coming over to me.

"Kind of," I said. Actually my girlfriend was a pretty cheerleader from our high school basketball days.

"Have you had sex with her?"

"I'll get this all out," I said. "Here we go, two martinis . . ."

"Or is she withholding herself for marriage?"

" . . . I'll open the bottle of wine . . ."

"I like sex," she said. "I love sex."

Pop! went the cork. "I figure you'll have the martinis first so I won't pour the wine," I said.

"Oh, I'm thirsty . . . and I am hungry, too, if you understand what I mean."

"Okay, your salad is here," I pointed. "Here is the main course, under this cover, and the dessert is inside the cart . . ."

"I like it inside," she said.

"To keep it cold," I said.

"Don't you like it hot?"

"It's ice cream," I said. "You don't want it to melt."

Look, I was not an idiot. I knew she was being seductive but, being a virgin, being trained to "respect women," as my mother taught me, and, truthfully, being terrified of a full grown, curvy, beautiful, sex crazed, and naked woman it overwhelmed me—so all I wanted to do was get the hell out of there. I wasn't prepared for this; I didn't even know what to do in the full sexual context if you want to know the truth. I knew how to kiss but all the other stuff—well I had actually never figured out yet what all the other stuff was.

Yes, I was in college; on a full academic scholarship; I was smart—but when it came to women, well, I knew nothing.

As I was running towards the door, she said, "You don't know what you're missing."

At the door I said, "Call housekeeping and they will get rid of the cart when you are done or put it in the hallway."

"Don't you want a tip?" she asked, but I was already out the door and galloping towards the elevators.

I didn't tell any of the other waiters, not because the story of a beautiful naked woman trying to lure me into sex wasn't highly interesting; I just didn't want them to know how lame I was.

The Five Towns on Long Island is composed of Lawrence, Cedarhurst, Hewlett, Woodmere and Inwood. Frankly, I had never heard of this place when I was a freshman in college. Growing up in Brooklyn, I thought of Long Island as a distant place, known as "the country" to my family. Strangely enough, six years later I would be working at Lawrence High School but I obviously didn't know that then.

There were six people at the table, three men, three women, all of them well dressed, but two of the women had face lifts that were so horrifying that it took all my strength of will not to just stand there and gape.

All of them ordered steaks.

"I'll have mine medium well," said the brunette stretch-faced woman.

"I'll have medium," said the bleached-blonde stretch-face.

"I hate it medium," said the normal woman. "Make my filet mignon well done."

The men all ordered rare porter house steaks.

"We are from the FIVE TOWNS," proudly announced the normal looking woman.

"Ah, oui," I said, finishing up the writing of the last order.

"Do you know where the Five Towns is?" asked the bleached-blonde stretch-face.

"After zee four towns?" I smiled.

"Do not be obnoxious!" scolded the brunette stretch-face.

"A joke," I said.

"It wasn't funny young man," said the normal woman.

"Sorry," I said and walked to the kitchen.

"The French are all obnoxious," said the bleached-blonde stretch-face.

In the kitchen when you have such multiple steak orders for one table you arrange them in a way that you can tell which is which.

At the table, the FIVE TOWNS women continued to drive me nuts.

"Mine does not look to be well done," said the normal one.

"I asked for medium rare and this is too well done," said the brunette stretch-face.

"This is not medium, this is well done," said the bleached-blonde stretch-face.

I spoke to the brunette stretch-face, "Madame, you ordered a medium-well filet mignon, not medium rare. I wrote it right here."

"You made a mistake when you wrote it down," she said. "Take it back and do it right."

I took the steak from her.

"Take mine back and cook it some more," said the normal woman.

"Monsieurs are your steaks okay?" I asked.

"Great."

"Fine."

"Delicious."

I took the two steaks back to the kitchen. Chef Joseph did not like to redo an order; he felt it an insult for someone to send something back to him because he felt he always got everything right the first time.

"You have to heat zis one up more," I said. "She sez it eezn't well done."

Chef Joseph cut a little into it. "It's well done enough," he said.

"She sez it eezn't," I said.

"It is," he said.

"But she sez . . ."

"Fuck her. Give it to her again. Put it under the heat lamp to make it seem more cooked," said Chef Joseph. I put it under the heat lamp.

"Zis one, she screwed up her order. She vanted medium rare but she ordered medium vell," I said. My accent seemed to be taking on a German tinge.

"You fucked up?"

"No," I said. "I didn't. I know vhat she ordered."

"Throw the fucking steak out!" he screamed.

While Chef Joseph put in a new steak, I brought the re-heated one back to the table and put it in front of the brunette stretched-faced woman. She cut it and nodded, "That is much, much better. Now it's well done. You got it right this time." The steak looked exactly as it had before—but you never argue with diners!

"And how ez everyone doing?" I asked of the men.

"Great."

"Fine."

"Delicious."

I went back into the kitchen and got the medium rare one to bring out. At the table I placed it in front of the bleached-blonde stretch-face.

"This is too well done," she said after cutting it.

"Vhat?" I asked.

"Send it back, my God, can't you people get anything right?" she sniffed.

In the kitchen I stood there with the plate in hand. Chef Joseph turned his baleful gaze at me.

"She sez it is too vell done now," I said.

"Tell her to fuck herself," he said.

"She vants you to cook another," I said.

"Give it to me," he said. I did. He looked at it.

"It's cooked perfectly," he said. I shrugged. He cooked another steak.

I delivered it to the table and placed it before the bleached-blonde stretch-face. She looked up at me. "Do you realize that everyone is almost finished with their meals and I am just starting?"

"Yes, oui, Madame," I said.

"You can't seem to get your act together in this place, can you?" she scolded.

"No," I said.

She started to eat, put her fork down, handed me the plate and said, "Tell the chef that he should consider another occupation. Take this garbage back and I do not intend to pay for it."

I took the plate back. I stood there with it in my hand. Chef Joseph came over, took the plate from my hand, looked at the steak, and then looked at me.

"She said it vas garbage," I said. The whole kitchen went silent. The chef took the steak off the plate and threw it in my face . . . *and I punched him.* Then we were rolling, punching, and scrambling all over the kitchen floor, knocking over the vat of beef bourguignon all over ourselves and when that happened we stopped.

Chef Joseph was tired. I was tired. We were both filthy, coated with beef bourguignon.

"You didn't do it," he said, catching his breath. "I shouldn't have thrown the steak at you."

"I shouldn't have punched you," I said.

"Don't charge any of them; just tell them to leave," he said, getting up.

I got up, wiped my face and hands off with a towel and asked one of the waitresses if she would tell the table to leave, no charge. She was kind enough to do so.

I watched from between a small opening in a curtain at the back of the restaurant near the kitchen.

"We are from the FIVE TOWNS!" shouted the bleached-blonde stretch-face.

"We are from the Five Towns!" shouted the brunette stretch-face.

"Let's go," said a husband.

"Come on," said the other husband.

"Out," said the third husband, taking some money from his wallet.

"What are you doing?" shouted the normal woman.

"I'm leaving the waiter a tip," said the husband. "It's not his fault."

"Put that money away," she yelled. "These people don't deserve tips. They should all be fired."

And I was soon fired after this; but not for that.

I made a big error, an error that got me fired on the spot by the general manager of the restaurants. Here's the story:

The manager came to the employees' area of the restaurant after a particularly trying evening.

"Everyone, listen up," he said. "I just fired the breakfast cook today. Tomorrow is Saturday and I need a cook for breakfast. Any of you know how to cook?"

No one said anything but each and every one of us looked at each and every one of us.

"How much dooz it pay?" I asked.

"Ten bucks an hour," he said.

"Oh, yez, I haf verked as a kook," I said.

"Report tomorrow morning at five thirty. You get paid from the very beginning; from 5:30 until noon. Not bad right?"

"Oui," I said.

At 5:30 I was there. The manager fitted me with a long white apron and put the big chef's hat on my head.

"Good luck," he said. "You look good. Any problems you just call me, okay."

"Oui," I said.

"Oh, I forgot, our waitress called in last night. She's sick. You'll have to wait the tables too," he threw this over his shoulder as he left the café.

Cooking and waiting on tables—I was in for some good money this morning if I could pull it off. How hard could it be to make breakfast?

In the café breakfast was cooked in front of everyone at a giant grill. I looked around to familiarize myself with the area.

Then I decided to arrange things in my station so I could find them easily. The very first thing, I cut my thumb on a knife I tried to move from here to there. So I went into the gourmet restaurant next door, went to the first aid box, took a band aid and some iodine, which I slathered on my thumb, and then I put the band aid on. I hoped that would be the worst thing that would happen to me this morning.

It wasn't.

Back in the café's exposed kitchen, I checked out the limited menu instead of trying to arrange things that could cut me up some more. Okay, not bad, I knew how to cook everything except Eggs Benedict. What the hell were those? I had to make diners not order that or I'd be in deep water.

Bingo! I made up small table tents with "Monsieur Scobe's Saturday's Special!" Under that I put, "Hot, Delicious, Pancakes!" That should steer people towards something I could make with ease. Pancakes would be a breeze. I'd seen my mother make pancakes hundreds of times.

I made pancake batter in a giant pot and waited for my first customers to arrive. At 6:15 a couple came in—the beginning of the end of my career as a chef.

"May I help vous? We haf great pancakes," I said in my best French accent.

"No, no," said the woman, "I'll have Eggs Benedict, please."

"Me too," said the man.

"Zee pancakes are excellent," I said, kissing my fingers to the sky.

"Naw," said the man.

"Oh, I zink you will loff them," I said.

"Eggs Benedict," she said. "I hate pancakes. I had food poisoning once with pancakes."

"I assure you Madame, our pancakes will not do that to vous, I assure vous of zat," I said.

"Eggs Benedict," he said.

"As vous wish," I said bowing.

I went to my kitchen area. Eggs Benedict? Christ! Maybe I could bluff my way out of this one. I went back to the couple's table.

"We seem to be out of benedicts," I said, smiling.

"Very funny," laughed the husband. "I am sure they will be delicious."

"Ha! Ha!" I laughed and went back to my kitchen. I zipped away for a moment and went to the front desk of the hotel. There was a young woman receptionist.

"Do you know how to make Eggs Benedict?" I asked.

"Are you the chef?" she asked.

"Yes," I said. "It's my first day and how to make those just slipped my mind—I'm so nervous."

"Yeah, they are simple; I eat them all the time," she said.

"What are you doing?" asked the manager coming up behind me.

"I, uh," I said.

"He's asking me how to make Eggs Benedict," said the receptionist.

"What?" he said.

"I want to make sure it is, ez, the same in America az it ez in Paris," I said.

"Well, we use two halves of English muffin, with ham or bacon, poached eggs and hollandaise sauce," said the receptionist.

"Poached eggs, ah, ha, and in America how do you do that exactly?" I asked.

"Boil them in water until the whites are hard and the center is soft," said the manager. "It's the same in Paris for God's sake."

"Ah, but of course," I said.

I hurried back into the café, boiled some water, cracked four eggs and dumped them into the water. I toasted two English muffins; fried some bacon, and then 12 Japanese diners came in—kids and adults.

"Zit wherever you vish!" I called to them as I scoured the cabinets for some hollandaise sauce. They moved several tables together and they all sat down. I heard them chattering as they held up the table tent. *Please, God, let them order pancakes.*

I found the hollandaise, dumped the eggs on the English muffins, put the bacon on top, said a little prayer, and served the couple. Then I ran back and got them orange juice and coffee.

"Oh, my God!" screamed the wife as I poured her coffee.

"Yez?" I said.

She held a bloody band aid up. I looked at my thumb; my band aid must have fallen into the Eggs Benedict.

I took the band aid from her. "I vuz looking for zat," I said. "Do you like vous eggs, sir?" I asked the man. He gazed at me as if I were crazy.

He stood up; his wife stood up. They both threw their napkins on the table and stormed out of the café.

I looked over at the Japanese table. "Americans!" I said, throwing my hands up. "They are never satisfied! When vous come from Japan, as vous do," I added. "Vous understand the meaning of being satisfied."

"We're from California," said one man. "I've never set foot in Japan."

"My family has been in this country for over a hundred years," said a woman.

"Ah," I said. "And vaht vould you like for breakfast?" I asked.

"We have all decided," said the older man. "Pancakes for everyone! The Scobe Specials, okay?"

Thank you, Jesus!

"Yes, oui, oui," I said.

"Daddy, he said wee-wee," said one of the little girls.

"The word yes in French sounds like wee, so yes is wee," said one of the women.

"So when they go to make number one they say 'yes, yes'?"

"No," said the woman. "Sir?" she called over to me.

"Oui?"

"How do you say urinate in French?" she asked.

"What? I mean, vhat?" I asked.

"Urinate in French," said the woman.

Well, she obviously didn't speak French and I assumed all the others didn't either. So I took a shot at it. "Urinatetwa," I said confidently.

"Urinatetwa," nodded the little girl.

I smiled and hoped she'd never visit France.

I stirred the pancake batter and then made 36 big pancakes on the big grill—three big ones for each of them—the Scobe Saturday Specials. Then the pancakes started to spread out on the grill like crazy. I had forgotten that pancake batter spreads when it is being cooked, but I had made each one so large that the spreading looked as if the Blob were attacking earth.

When finished the pancakes were humongous; so much so that they couldn't fit on the plates without totally flopping off. How the hell would I serve these?

A serving tray—a giant one!—that would solve the problem. I'd put all the pancakes piled to the sky on it—*family-style* eating at its best.

So that's what I did.

First I brought out plates to everyone; then gave them the maple syrup, and then I brought over the gigantic serving tray piled high with monstrously large pancakes and put it in the middle of the table—moving everything out of the way in order to fit it.

"Deeg in," I said.

"These are on a dirty tray," said one of the kids.

"Here let me cut these for vous," I said to distract everyone from the kid's comment. Shit, I *had* forgotten to wash the damn tray. It *was* filthy.

"We are leaving," said the oldest man.

Everyone got up and headed for the door.

"Other zhan ze dirt, what ez ze matter?" I called after them.

The manager came in four minutes later and fired me, not only as the cook but as a waiter too. My waitering career lasted seven months; my cooking career lasted two hours.

15

The Man with Cape and Hat

Bless me father for I have sinned. I stole and befriended a drug dealer.

He was a paper clip man, four-feet tall, made from thousands of paper clips I took from the storeroom. He had an aluminum foil cape going from both shoulders to the ground and an aluminum foil cowboy hat. I called him *The Man with Cape and Hat*. It took me just three weeks to build my work of art which then got me fired from my first fulltime adult job. And the executives of the insurance company wouldn't even let me take my creation home. They kept him.

Within a week of graduating college I got a job at a famous insurance company in Manhattan. I had to wear a jacket and tie each day and my desk was situated in the middle of hundreds of desks where new workers or those workers who had not even made it to the lowest form of management "slaved" away—if slaving away meant doing almost nothing all day. Small management types, mostly fidgety, hyper-type-A personalities, had very small enclosed offices along that floor's walls where they fidgeted hoping for advancement off this floor to a higher level.

The big executives were on higher floors and the biggest executive bosses of all executive bosses existed in the rarified atmosphere at the top of this 50 story building on Wall Street.

Unfortunately, there wasn't all that much work to do at my level of the company which was on the 39th floor; which everyone called "Peasantville."

My task put me in charge of insuring bus fleets in Texas. Other than a few mailings back and forth a few times a week, with maybe a couple of phone calls thrown in, my real work day started at 10AM, when the Texas offices opened, and ended at about 10:40 AM. From 9AM to 10AM, I drank coffee and stared at walls or at the pretty women as they wiggled past my desk to the coffee machine and water fountain.

After my Texas work, the rest of the day I had to "look like you are working, goddamn it, Frank or they will watch all of us" according Cigarette Sam—otherwise known as Cigsam—a loud pain in the ass who thought he knew everything, except he didn't seem to know that cigarette smoking would kill him.

Cigsam got that name because he smoked four packs of unfiltered Lucky Strikes per day; you could plainly see his fingers yellowed from the myriad tars oozing out from those mini chimneys. He had a deathly pallor and a twitchy face and, at 35 years old, he had been passed over for promotions for the past 13 years. He was going nowhere in the company; he knew it, everyone else knew it, too, but he also didn't want to be thrown out the front door either because he had a wife and two ugly children. So Cigsam had developed an expertise in "pretending to work hard" although he was given almost no assignments by the fidgety executives in the side offices by the time I had arrived.

No one liked him because he had the personality of one of his cigarettes—hot with sticky tars. He was also a clinger, a person who trapped you in order to converse with you for endless hours about how much he knew and how stupid everyone else was.

The desk that actually smacked up against mine was inhabited by a total druggie nicknamed Doctor Timothy J. Leary in honor of that wacky psychopathic psychologist who pushed LSD as the way to inner salvation and esoteric knowledge and whose ashes now supposedly float in outer space where his brain went many decades before he actually died. We called our druggie Timjay for short. And Timjay was in fact short, maybe five feet two inches, and skinny as a side show performer, severely hunched over with bloodshot, somewhat vacant eyes and a slight stammer when he was ripped out of his mind, which was, frankly, every day.

Yes, skinny Timjay was stoned from the moment he entered the building in the morning to the moment he floated out on his personal cloud at five o'clock. He smoked joints all day, going to his "hidden chamber," which was the cleanup closet for the night janitors, and you could smell the marijuana smoke reeking on him and wafting from under the clean-up closet when he was in there toking away, but no one said anything because half the floor bought their pot from Timjay and, besides, he was a likeable fella.

Occasionally he took pills of various varieties. Timjay was the first person to explain to me that you could swallow certain cough concoctions that then acted like speed in your system and that the cough medicine combination kept him awake because the pot and pills tended to put him to sleep. He was always asking me if I wanted to get high because "this place sucks and what else is there to do? Smoke some joints, check out the ladies' butts, and eat. What more is there to life?" Timjay did eat all day long—dozens of candy bars that he had stocked in every drawer of his desk.

While I had little to do, true, I also didn't want to be sailing the waves of altered consciousness while working just in case someone who could fire me saw me starring at elephants parading through Peasantville.

Timjay didn't care about being fired and he didn't care about working and so he actually didn't work. He gave his work to Cigsam, paying him a small fee, since Cigsam also had nothing to do. But Cigsam was a rat of the first order by this time in his life and so he delighted in running to the small executives whose small offices lined the walls and telling these small executives in those small wall offices "that drug addict does nothing; I have to do his work to cover for him! Can you imagine that?" Cigsam hoped that this information would help him finally get a promotion to a wall office, something his tar-filled lungs truly cherished. In fact, many of the fidgety wall office executives also bought their drugs from Timjay so no one was going to recommend that their personal supplier be fired. Timjay had some of the best pot in all of Manhattan and you didn't have to deal with the street scum to get it either. What was better than buying great pot right in your own office?

So poor yellow-fingered Cigsam sat at his desk, cigarette smoke billowing out of him and into the air all around us (you could smoke indoors in those days), and this poor sap had no idea that every time he ran to rat out Timjay "the addict," he was in fact annoying the hell out of those he spoke to who kept thinking they would like to recommend Cigsam for termination and not their likeable drug peddler.

Now, I am not the laid back B-personality type; I'm type A all the way. I tend to enjoy working or at least enjoy working what I liked to work, or at the very, very least I enjoyed being active, so when I had to "pretend to be working," my idle hands became the Devil's workshop, as the Sisters of Charity used to constantly say.

To have something challenging to do, Timjay and I decided to become an airport by making paper airplanes and flying them out of the windows of our old building where many of the windows actually opened—especially the ones in the stairwells.

At first we'd make a couple of planes each and then head to the stairwell and launch them. Since we were 39 floors high those planes caught the wind currents and flew beautifully.

After a week of this, I said to Timjay, "Why don't we set an all-time record and launch thousands of them?"

I remember when Jake "the Snake" Jacobsen decided to set the all-time world record at Our Lady of Angels in 7th Grade and our whole class made thousands of planes and flew them out of the windows when big, vicious Brother Lucas wasn't watching. By the way, we called everything a "world record" if it were a big enough event whether there was such a thing as a world record for that activity or not.

Timjay was excited, "Groovy," he said as he ate his fourth Hershey Bar of the day.

So we took reams of stationary out of the storeroom without anyone seeing us; doing this over a two-week period, and we started crafting our planes. When we left work we'd put the finished planes in boxes in a totally empty, walk-in closet the company had forgotten about. Timjay had somehow gotten the key from one of his small executive drug buyers for the closet and we now thought of that space as belonging to us.

When we had approximately four thousand planes, we took the boxes of them to the stairwell. We actually drafted help from some of the other whacked-out workers. We opened the window and started throwing the planes out. The swirling, powerful Wall Street winds picked them up and the planes flew this way and that; some up, some down, some straight away. Within 10 minutes the streets were littered with planes and people were beginning to look up and around to see where this barrage came from.

"We have to dump the remainder all at once," I said. "People are really looking around."

So we dumped the contents of several boxes out the window; a couple of thousand planes sailed the winds all at once. The air was filled with them; the people on the streets were actually cheering now. No one had ever seen so many paper planes in their lives. It was like a ticker-tape-plane parade.

The very next day, one of the big bosses from the floor under the top floor called a meeting of our floor in one of the largest board rooms on the 49th floor.

"We know that these paper planes came from one of the offices somewhere on the mid-floors based on eyewitness reports," said one big executive from the stratosphere level of the company.

"Anyone who knows who did this should report the culprits to us immediately for us to take proper action," said a sour-faced lady executive, smartly dressed in a suit. "There is a reward for the person or people who turn in those who have embarrassed our company. We don't want something like this to ever happen again."

"How do you know it was one of our employees who did this?" asked one of our small executives.

"Eye witnesses and it was our stationary with our name on it," said the big male executive.

"Oh," said the questioner.

When the meeting was over, Cigsam sprinted to the big executives of the 49th floor, his cigarette dangling out of his mouth, ashes falling on his suit, excitedly introducing himself to them, and now I could see him pointing to Timjay and to me as we left the board room. He nodded up and down like a bobble-head doll, talking furiously. Both of the big executives stared over at us and nodded slowly, seriously.

Timjay and I were called into the big male executive's office the next morning. The last face I saw as I went to the elevators was Cigsam sitting there smoking and smirking.

"That fuck actually turned us in," said Timjay.

"Just say no to everything. No explanations. I'll do the talking if we have to talk," I said.

"Groovy," he said. He was so stoned that this was just an adventure for him.

"Wipe your lips, you have chocolate on them," I said.

After a fifteen minute wait outside the big male executive's office on the 49th floor, we were ushered in by his pretty secretary. "Sit down you two." We sat. "We have received word that you two were the people who sent all those paper planes all over the city yesterday," said the big executive eyeing us.

"No," I said.

"No," said Timjay.

"No?" asked the big executive. He looked surprised that we had said "no."

"No," I said.

"No," said Timjay.

"No, really?" said the big executive.

"No."

"No."

"No?"

"No."

"No."

"Then why would this person who has worked for us for a very long time tell us that it was you two guys who did it?"

"I don't know," I said.

"I don't know," said Timjay.

"You don't know?" asked the executive.

"No."

"No."

"Could you be lying to me?"

"No."

"No."

"How do I solve my problem?" asked the executive.

"Ask the managers on our floor who they believe—us or the person who claims we did it," I said.

"Yeah," said Timjay.

"Ask a bunch of them to get a good cross-section of opinion," I said. "You'll be able to see what they think of us, and what they think of the person who claims it was us who did this." A cross-section of the small wall-office executives would be at least 50 percent in our favor since they bought their drugs from Timjay and all the small wall executives couldn't stand Cigsam. The odds were in our favor in a big way.

The executive nodded. "Okay, okay," he said. "You are dismissed . . . for now."

Two days later, a red-faced Cigsam came to our desks with the sour-faced female boss. Cigsam had his head bowed.

"You have something to say to these fine young men?" asked the sour-faced female executive.

"Yes," said Cigsam. "I want to apologize because I thought it was the two of you who did the airplane thing the other day."

"Well, thank you very much," Timjay said. "Would you like a Peanut Butter Cup?" Cigsam ignored the offer.

"Thank you," I said.

"You two young men please continue your fine jobs," said the sour-faced female executive.

"And you," said the sour-faced female executive to Cigsam, "are on notice not to spread such nasty rumors again."

"Yes, miss, miz, ma'am, uh, yes, of course, yes," said a visibly shaken Cigsam. I looked over at the small executives' offices along the walls and many of these people were laughing and gloating about the public humiliation of Cigsam. They must have given the executives earfuls of bad reports on Cigsam and they must have invented great lies to say about Timjay and me.

It turns out that many of the small executives had gotten together and decided to tell the executives that they actually thought Cigsam had floated all those planes because he had "cracked up." They also told the executives that Timjay was a fine worker that the unstable Cigsam had a deep-seated hatred of him for reasons unknown to them. They said that Timjay was the kind of worker the company needed to continue its great traditions into the future. All of them were high on Timjay, they proclaimed. Actually, most of them were high, period. They buried the executives in piles of bullshit.

That got us out of that mess and Timjay went back to his usual stoned indifference. Cigsam became somewhat insane now in his hatred of Timjay. He'd spend the day sneering at him and cursing Timjay under his foul breath. Timjay stopped shipping out his work to Cigsam too. That left Cigsam with absolutely nothing to do all day but hatch his plans against Timjay.

Cigsam didn't like me too much either but his burning hatred of Timjay was so fierce that he couldn't really be bothered with me . . . that is, until the creation of *The Man with Cape and Hat*.

By my second month of "looking as if I were working," which was mid-July, I was like a crab in a box. I couldn't stand working there, I mean, *not working* there. So one day at my desk I composed a letter to one of the bus fleets I was insuring in Texas but I wrote it in a Texas drawl—the down-home variety. I sent the letter out but all letters had copies registered with the secretarial pool. Three days later, at 10:40AM, a big boss called me upstairs to the 49th floor and when I entered his giant office he held up a copy of my letter.

"What is this letter?" he asked.

"It's to my account in Texas," I said innocently.

"You wrote it in some kind of dialogue," he said.

"You mean dialect?" I asked.

"Don't be a wise ass with me," he said. "This is not a professional letter. This is an insult to the company you sent it to."

The phone rang. The executive sat down behind his desk, continuing to hold the copy of my letter in his hand—in fact, he waved it at me.

"Sir," interrupted the secretary. "Sorry to disturb you but there is a call from . . ." she looked at me sorrowfully, "Texas."

"If we lose this account; you lose your job," the executive said to me.

"Hello, Dan here," said the executive. "Yes, Mr. Reynolds, yes, he is actually in here right now . . . I can assure you that we . . . what? Really? Ha! Ha! Yep . . . well, yes, sir, we do encourage creativity here . . . yes, yes, he is a smart young man." The executive put my letter on his desk. "And we are very proud that he works for us . . . certainly, I'll put you in touch with our cab fleet division . . . well, thank *you* . . . a pleasure to do business with you Mr. Reynolds . . . hang on and I will connect you."

He pushed a button, "Sarah, connect Mr. Reynolds with our cab division."

He hung up. He stared at his desk for a few moments. Then he looked at me.

"You are a very lucky young man. Mr. Reynolds, the owner of the bus fleet, he thought your letter was great and complimented us on having workers such as you on our staff."

"That's great," I said. "Is there something about cabs too?"

"Yes," said the big executive, the muscles on his jaw working. "He's switching from another insurance company to us because of your creativity. He thinks we don't act like the normal insurance company and he likes that."

I nodded gravely. "Mmmm, I see," I said. "You were saying to me before he called?" I said innocently.

"I am saying to you now that you were lucky this time," said the big executive. "Don't press your luck."

I *pressed* my luck.

I was sitting doing nothing and I picked up a paper clip; opened it; bent it this way and that, then took another paper clip, opened it, bent it and attached it to the first one. And that was the start of *The Man with Cape and Hat*.

At first I just worked on the head. I figured I'd put the head in the outer corner of my desk as many of the employees had trinkets or pictures of family members or significant others on their desks.

I must now make a confession that I have never told anyone. I couldn't get the clips to always fit without them falling apart or collapsing the whole damn project. So I resorted to little drops of strong adhesive. This allowed me to bend and mold without really having to worry about whether the paper clips could actually hold what I was creating.

All right I was not Michelangelo or Leonardo DaVinci—but I was still an artist, creating something that had never been created before; a man with cape and hat made from paper clips and aluminum foil (and, okay, some glue).

I finished the head in a few days. It wasn't hard. I had about six hours of free time at work so I spent most of it feverishly working on the statue.

"Hey, man, that head looks groovy," said Timjay. "You know, man, why not do a whole body too?"

A whole body, hmmm, that would be some challenge.

So I went about it.

I knew I couldn't do the whole body at my desk as Cigsam was now watching me closely since I finished the head.

He came over to me once as I was finishing the head. "I hope those paper clips are not from the company."

"No," I said.

"No," Timjay added.

"Was I talking to you?" asked Cigsam.

"No," said Timjay undisturbed. "But I was talking to you Mister Cigsam."

"Cigsam is not my name, you drug addict," said Cigsam.

"I am going to tell them upstairs that you are harassing me," said Timjay.

Cigsam's face turned flushed.

"I bought these," I lied. "I would never waste the company's money on a few paper clips."

"Go away and shove your head into a urinal," said Timjay unwrapping a Mounds bar.

Cigsam smirked and went back to his desk to Lucky Strike himself to death.

I decided to use the empty closet where we made those thousands of planes. I brought in boxes of paper clips and began the mighty task of creating a full body upon which I could place the beautiful paper-clip head. I had not yet thought of the capstone for my project, the actual cape and hat, but the body-work went magnificently.

The only thing that slowed me down was the constant annoyance of Cigsam who kept walking over to my desk to ask the ENTIRE

EARTH in his irritatingly loud voice, "Where's that Scoboletie guy? He isn't at his desk again. Anyone seen him?"

Almost everyone ignored the despised Cigsam but Timjay always came up with something witty to say like, "Fuck you!" or "Go away dick face!"

I spent about half the day in the closet working on my piece de résistance. When the body was done I put the head on it and the whole thing crashed to the ground. It couldn't stand up on its own. When it crashed a few of the paper clips were jettisoned out of the man but they were easy to glue back into place.

I put a wooden support behind him to make sure he didn't come crashing down in the future. As I was working on the support I kept thinking *this man needs something to complete him*. I then realized that if I put a cape and a hat on him, my paper clip man would be distinct, unique, and beautiful. So I brought some aluminum foil in to work and on the final day of work (and of my job too) I dressed my man.

At 11 o'clock Timjay and I called to attention everyone on our floor, including our small wall executives to make our presentation.

"Ladies and gentlemen . . . and Cigsam," yelled Timjay. "Frank Scoblete, known to his friends as Scobe, now our resident Van Gogh, is now ready to unveil his great work of art, *The Man with Cape and Hat!*" I walked from the closet onto the main floor, carrying my work of art.

"We can't see it," yelled some of the folks in the back of the room. So I climbed up on a desk and Timjay handed me *The Man with Cape and Hat*. The entire room howled its approval. I bowed.

"This great work of art is my finest work," I yelled. Everyone clapped. That was due more to Timjay handing out free joints to anyone who desired one and I could see that half the workers on the floor were stoned out of their minds, many of them devouring donuts.

"This work of art is called *The Man with Cape and Hat!* And he is dedicated to all of you hard workers . . ." I started.

"Except Cigsam!" yelled Timjay.

I didn't see Cigsam when I looked around.

"I am going to put *The Man with Cape and Hat!* by the water cooler so that all of you will be inspired when you wet your whistle!" I announced.

The workers erupted into wild shouts of joy and encouragement. They sounded like prisoners being released from a gulag.

I jumped off the desk and carried *The Man with Cape and Hat!* to the water cooler. The cheers and screams stopped suddenly. The small executives in the wall offices catapulted back inside and busied themselves with whatever they did. Everyone else leaped back to their desks too.

It was Cigsam, leading one of the 49th floor big executives into Peasantville. Cigsam triumphantly pointed to *The Man with Cape and Hat!*

Since I was standing right next to my work, Cigsam pointed to me, "He did it. His name is Frank Scoboletie . . ."

"Scoblete," I corrected.

"And I think he stole all those paper clips!" smirked Cigsam. "And he's friends with that druggie over there!" he pointed to Timjay who was lazily munching on a donut. Timjay gave Cigsam the finger when the big executive turned to look at the paper clip man.

"Come with me to my office," said the big executive. "Take this thing with you."

I picked up *The Man with Cape and Hat!* and followed the big executive.

"Do you want me to come too?" asked Cigsam.

The executive looked at him as if Cigsam were a worm (which to me he was), "No," he said. "You can get back to work."

As we entered the elevator an eruption of boos came from the 39th floor. Timjay called out, "Kill Cigsam!" and there was a loud cheer.

I followed the big executive to his office. "Sit in the waiting room," he said. I sat down with *The Man with Cape and Hat!* in front of me.

"That's very pretty," said the pretty secretary.

"Thanks," I said. "It's called *The Man with Cape and Hat!*"

About 15 minutes later, the big executive came out. "We're going upstairs," he said. My Lord, I would be the first person from the 39th floor who actually got to go to the 50th floor where the bosses of all bosses held sway.

I had to wait another 15 minutes in a boss-of-all-bosses waiting area, again with my creation standing in front of me.

"What's that?" asked the secretary.

"*The Man with Cape and Hat!*" I said.

"Did you make that?"

"Yes."

"Very interesting," she said.

In the office, the boss of all bosses and the big executive boss from the 49th floor were seated at a big table in an office the size of a basketball court. One side of the room was a desk that you could probably sail across the Atlantic Ocean on and the other side of the room, where we were, had the big long table with chairs all around it.

I stood there holding *The Man with Cape and Hat!*

"Sit down," said the boss of all bosses. "Mr. Thomas here has told me that you spent your working time making this . . ." he indicated my creation . . ."thing?"

"Yes," I said.

"You understand that we are not paying people to make such things?"

"Yes."

"I was told that you also used company property, paper clips, to make this object?" he asked.

"Yes."

"You understand what I must do now?" asked the boss of all bosses.

"Yes."

"I have to set an example for workers so that they know they are not here for fun and games but to work hard."

"Yes."

"As of today you are no longer employed at our company. Although you are technically being fired, we are giving you two weeks severance pay because a review of your record indicates that up until recently your work has been satisfactory."

"Thank you," I said.

"Well, that's it," he said. He leaned over the table and shook my hand. I stood up and took hold of *The Man with Cape and Hat!*

"No, no," said the boss of all bosses. "Leave that here. We own him because it was made with our paper clips."

"Yes, sir," I said.

As I left the office I heard the boss of all bosses say to the big executive, "I like this. I'm going to keep it here. What was the name that kid gave this?"

"The Man with Cape and Hat!" said the big executive.

16

Happy Home

Bless me father for I have sinned. I did not love my neighbors as myself.

After the horrifying, terrifying incident in visiting that mind-boggling, haunted house in Massapequa looking to buy my first home, which I describe in my book *The Virgin Kiss*, my first wife Lucille and I bought a house in Valley Stream, New York, a suburb which was only 25 miles as the pigeon flies to the Empire State Building.

This was 1977.

It was a big house, three floors, two bathrooms, three bedrooms; a giant living room, a nice-sized dining room, a great kitchen, a terrific playroom and at the very top a large room that I converted into an office where I would write my great works of literature, which I never did write.

The house cost $45,000—the cost of a decent car today.

It looked like a pleasant neighborhood too. All the properties were neatly kept; little kids played happily on the streets and my one year-old son, Gregory, would have plenty of childhood companions.

Our next door neighbors had a slightly bent "Happy-Home" sign plastered to their front door. Wow! A loving married couple proclaiming their devotion and joy. I saw very little of that kind of passion from most other married couples.

As we were moving in, a heavy-set woman of about 45 from the "Happy-Home" came over with brownies and sausages. I was just taking some stuff off the truck we had rented.

"Hello, new neighbors," said the woman.

"Hi," I said, getting down from the back of the truck. I shook her hand.

"Hi," said Lucille.

"Got you something to hold you over until you get settled," she said, handing me the two dishes.

I took the dishes from her and brought them into the house.

"My name is Jo Mantroni," she said rushing in right behind me. Lucille came in after her. "This house is just like mine only yours is bigger and has a top floor which I have never seen."

"Ah," I said.

"When we get in and get settled I'll take you up there," said Lucille.

"Oh, I'll just go up now and save you the trouble," said Jo Mantroni heading right for the stairs.

"It's a real mess up there," said Lucille.

But Jo Mantroni was already halfway up the staircase.

"She's kinda forward," I said.

"That's the suburbs I guess," said Lucille. "People are friendly."

"I guess, you know, Happy-Home," I said.

"It's a mess up here!" screamed Jo.

"We're just moving in; what does she expect?" I said to Lucille. She rolled her eyes.

"Don't get hurt!" I yelled up at her.

"Oh, I'm used to messes," she screamed.

Tonight was our first night in the new house. We put little Gregory to sleep; toasted ourselves with some wine and then, totally exhausted from a long day of work, we went to bed and fell into a deep sleep.

"Aaaaarrrrrggghhhhh! You fucking son of a bitch!"

I woke up with a start as did Lucille. My heart raced.

"I think I had a nightmare," I said.

"You goddamn cunt! Get out of my way, I'm going to kill him," came a man's voice from the Happy-Home driveway next door. The houses in this part of Valley Stream, known as Gibson, were very close together and this driveway was about five feet from our new house.

"What the hell?" asked Lucille.

"I am going to fucking kill you too," came the scream of a boy.

"You fucking kill me you fuck and you're dead you little fucking worm!" screamed the man.

"Put that screw driver down Perry that is your father talking!" screamed, yes, yes, it was . . . Jo Mantroni.

I looked over at the clock. It was 1AM.

"Mommy shut the fuck up I am trying to sleep!" screamed a girl.

"I'm going for a job interview tomorrow, could you fucking idiots keep it down?" screamed another girl.

"Perry you're twelve fucking years old!" screamed Jo Mantroni. "You should respect your fucking father!"

"He's a fucking moron!" screamed the 12-year-old son. He sounded as if he were right under our window. I didn't want to look out the window in case one of them fired a gun.

"I'll kill you for that!" screamed the father, and this was followed by loud bangs of stuff being thrown.

"You'll kill your own fucking son," screamed Jo.

"Should we call the police?" asked Lucille.

"The phone isn't connected yet," I said as this was long before the invention of the cell phone. "Someone else will probably call. Jesus Christ what the hell is the matter with those people?"

The brawl lasted another 10 minutes and then they went back into the house where I could hear some dishes smashing, a smattering of "fucks," and then silence.

I fell asleep around 4AM.

Bright and early, our doorbell rang. I went downstairs in my robe. Jo Mantroni stood there with another dish filled with scrambled eggs and bacon with toast on top.

"Good morning," she said cheerfully. "I figured you would be very tired from all that moving you did yesterday so I made you some breakfast. I hope you don't mind."

I took the dish from her.

"Thanks, uh, thanks for this," I said. I expected her to say something about the battle royal in her driveway last night but she never referred to it.

"We're going to Sacred Heart Church this morning," she said, waiting for me to say something because we had a long pause.

"Ah," I finally said. "Ah" is a great way to respond to people when you have no idea of how to actually respond.

My uncle has sex with sheep.

Ah.

Cindy has a penis.

Ah.

The Pope is an alien from Venus.

Ah.

"Are you two Catholic I hope?"

"Yes!" said Lucille behind me before I could shake my head "no" and tell Jo that we were lapsed Catholics, which really meant, "No, we gave that up."

Lucille was carrying little Gregory.

"Oh, good," said Jo. "I am the leader of the Ladies Auxiliary Prayer Conclave and I'd love you to join."

"Well, I, uh, with the new baby and, uh, you know," stammered Lucille.

"Nonsense," she said. "I have five children. Four of them are still living at home. You always have to make time for God. He made time for you in creating the world, didn't He?"

"Is the fifth one in college?" I asked to get the topic off God.

"No, he's institutionalized," said Jo.

"Ah," I said.

"Ah," said Lucille.

Thankfully at that moment Gregory started to cry. "He's hungry," said Lucille and whisked herself out of the doorway and into the house.

"Well," I said, "we'll love to eat this." I started to close the door.

"Are you going to church today?" she asked, putting her hand on the door to keep it from closing. "We'll drive you."

"Uh, we are going back to the church we went to in Far Rockaway," I lied.

"Which one is that?" she asked.

What the hell was the name of the church where we had Gregory baptized? That Baptism was a weird thing too. Father Haggerty, the priest who had to deal with Mary Louise's First Holy

Communion vomit-comet all over Our Lady of Angels church, was now the pastor of whatever the damn name of the church in Far Rockaway was where we baptized Gregory. That baptism we did so we could keep all the members of both sides of our families happy.

"Is it Saint Anthony?" she asked.

"Is Father Haggerty the pastor there?" I asked.

"No, Monsignor Carson is," she said.

"I guess it's early, I kinda forgot the name, ha, ha," I said.

"Saint Martin's," said Lucille behind me.

"I don't know that church," said Jo.

"Oh, it's a lovely little church," I said, then elaborated. "Beautiful stain glass windows."

"Well, I'll leave you two to it," said Jo. "Sunday is a wonderful day for being with your family isn't it?"

"Yeah," I said as I closed the door.

Sunday we spent working around the house; putting as much stuff away as possible. We went to bed exhausted at around nine o'clock.

"You mother-fucking cocksucker!" screamed a girl's voice in the driveway.

I was up in a second, heart thumping.

"You dumb cunt!" screamed a young man in the Mantroni driveway.

"Where the fuck have you two been?" screamed Mr. Mantroni. I hadn't yet learned his first name.

"Nowhere!" screamed the girl.

"Mr. Mantroni," started the young man. "We went to a movie and . . ."

"Fucking movies don't end at two o'clock in the morning you dumb fucking asshole," screamed Mr. Mantroni. "You're trying to get into my daughter's panties!"

"Oh, fuck that!" screamed the girl. "Fuck that! Fuck that!"

"Would everybody shut the fuck up!" screamed Jo, leaning out of her bedroom window on their side of the driveway. "Just shut the fuck up!"

"I am not trying to get into, well, you know," said the young man.

"The fuck you aren't!" screamed his girlfriend, the Mantroni girl. "All you want to do is fuck, fuck, fuck!"

"Have you had sexual relations *outside* of *marriage* with my daughter?" screamed Jo from her window. "Janet has he had sexual intercourse with you?"

"No, no," said the young man. I could now hear the quiver in his voice.

"I'll kill you if you ever do!" screamed Mr. Mantroni. "Yeah, run away you little fuck!"

I heard a car start up and I assumed that was the young man making his getaway. Then I heard things being thrown in the driveway.

"These fucking kids can drive you crazy!" screamed Mr. Mantroni. I peeked out the window then—and he threw a big tire iron down the driveway. It made it all the way into the street.

Monday morning I had to go to work. I taught English at Lawrence High School. This school was in the Five Towns—where that stretch-faced contingent lived.

"I'll see you," I said to my wife. I gave Gregory a big kiss. "You be good for mommy, Gregster."

"What if . . ." Lucille motioned with her head to indicate the Mantroni house. "What if she comes over again today?"

"You don't have to answer the door," I said.

"Oh, right, right." Lucille rolled her eyes.

"I don't know," I said. "Tell her you're busy or something. Tell her Gregory has the plague or something."

"You aren't helping," she said.

"I've got it better than you today," I laughed. "I only have to teach about a hundred fifty high school kids. You have to deal with the beasts of the night from next door."

After school when I pulled up to the house and turned into the driveway, Jo Mantroni was standing there.

"I want to get into the driveway," I said out the window of my car. She moved aside.

I parked the car in the driveway. We didn't have a garage; it had been converted into an outdoor sun house by the previous owners.

"I was waiting for you," said Jo as I got out of the car. "Lucille said you got home about 4PM but it is already," she checked her watch, "four-thirty. You're late."

"Well," I started. I was about to tell her that I had a meeting after school of the Science Fiction Club but then I thought, who the hell is *she?*

"So what's up?" I asked.

"Do you need some dirt?"

"What?"

"Dirt, dirt, for your garden in back; you have seen your garden, right? My husband Gary just came into a lot of dirt and he wants to get rid of it."

"No," I said. "I haven't even thought about the back yard yet."

"All of us in the neighborhood are proud of your garden and we want to make sure you keep it up. I love those flowers and all the colors."

"I'm not much of a gardener," I said walking towards the side door of my house.

"I can always help you," she said. "I like to get my hands dirty."

"Ah," I said, putting the key in the side door.

"Yep," she said smiling. She was gap-toothed, like the horny Wife of Bath from Geoffrey Chaucer's *The Canterbury Tales.*

"Okay, well," I said, "have a nice day."

"I'll see you tomorrow for dinner," she said.

"What?"

"Dinner tomorrow night," said Jo.

"Dinner?"

"Yes, you're off on Wednesday for a Jewish Holiday—don't those Jews have a lot of holidays? How do they ever get so rich being off so much?—and Lucille invited us over for dinner and to see your house now that you are in it."

"She did?" I asked that question as neutrally as I could. Inside I said something far different.

"Yes," said Jo, smiling. "Those last neighbors we had never invited us over. They never did. They weren't friendly at all. There was no neighborliness in them. The wife was a real drab. The husband was a good gardener but you couldn't even talk to him. He wouldn't even look at you. He always kept the windows shut too. I could see that from the driveway. You don't even have air-conditioning in that house. I didn't even know his wife had died except I read it in the church bulletin."

"Ah."

"But Lucille is different. I was telling her about those old owners and she immediately invited me over for tomorrow night's dinner when she realized that it was a Jewish holiday the next day and school was off for you and when I told her that she was really nice about us getting to be friends."

"Ah," I said.

"Yes, we'll have our whole family over; a good, home cooked meal."

"Ah," I said and closed the door.

"Lucille! Lucille!" I yelled as I entered the house.

"Upstairs!" she shouted back.

I ran upstairs to Gregory's room. She was changing Greg—at one year of age his pooh-poohs smelled just like shit.

"Woe, man, *woe*," I said holding my nose as I entered his room. "God, whew."

"If you changed him once in awhile you'd get used to the smell," she said.

"Did you invite Jo Mantroni and her whole family over for dinner tomorrow night?" I asked.

Lucille looked up at me. "She invited herself."

"What?" I asked.

"She just made it *sound* as if I invited her."

"And her whole family too?" I asked.

"Except the institutionalized one," nodded Lucille.

"What are you going to make?"

"We're ordering pizza," said Lucille. "I haven't even unpacked the pots and all the dishes yet."

"She said we were having a home cooked meal," I said.

"We can tell her the pizza was home cooked before they delivered it to us," said Lucille.

"Why the hell did you do this? These people aren't normal."

"Look," she said finishing dressing Greg who looked really content as she put him down in the crib. "She was blabbing about the last neighbors here and how unfriendly they were and how she thought the husband killed the wife."

"What? Do you think that's true?"

"No, I asked the O'Connors about that . . ."

"Who?" I asked.

"The O'Connors, next door," she indicated the other side of our house. "He's a retired principal and she's a homemaker. They have twelve kids."

"Twelve kids!"

"But they are only in contact with ten of them. Mrs. O'Connor said there are always a couple of rotten eggs in a dozen."

"Ah," I said.

"Mrs. O'Connor said no one was murdered; the wife died from a heart attack. She was eighty-five years old. The husband's son is the one who inherited the house when his father died and that's the person who sold us the house."

"So there was no murder, right?"

"Right," said Lucille. "And I *am* ordering pizza."

"She told me she was amazed that they kept the windows closed," I said.

"Yeah, well, so will we if every night they are out there."

"We got the phone today?" I asked.

"Yes."

"If they go at it tonight we call the cops," I said.

"You mother-fucker! I don't want that stupid thing in the house. It smells!" yelled the son, Perry Mantroni, somewhere on the driveway.

I turned over in bed and looked at the clock. It was 12:30AM. I reached for the phone.

"I took the stupid thing into the house," said one of the sisters.

"You stupid fuck!" yelled Jo Mantroni. "Get that thing out of my house! Now!"

I dialed 911.

"Nine-one-one, can I help you?"

"Yes, my next door . . ."

"What is your name sir?" asked the operator.

"Frank Scoblete," I said. "I live next to . . ."

"Spaghetti? Is this some kind of joke?"

"You idiot fuck! That thing could have rabies!" yelled Mr. Mantroni right under my bedroom window—my *open* bedroom window.

"You called me an idiot fuck?" asked the 911 operator.

"No, no, that's what I am calling about," I said.

"You are calling because I am an idiot fuck, sir?" asked the operator.

"Those are my neighbors," I said.

"They are idiot fucks too then?" asked the operator.

"You can't have a dog!" screamed Jo Mantroni, now also somewhere right below my window. "But you have to give it a bath right now!"

"Is that your wife screaming?" asked the operator.

"No, that's my neighbor's wife."

"Why is your neighbor's wife screaming in your house?" asked the operator.

"She isn't in my house . . ."

"You're in her house?" asked the operator.

"Forget it," I said. "Just forget it."

"Thank you for calling nine-one-one."

I hung up.

It was the evening of the home-made ordered-out delivered pizza and the Mantronies were a half hour late. The pizzas were in the kitchen, cooling off.

Ding-dong!

"Here they are," I said to myself.

Lucille came out of the kitchen.

I opened the door and there they were—THE MANTRONIES, except for the institutionalized one.

Mrs. Mantroni stood at the entrance and introduced each one.

"This is Perry, he's in eighth grade because he got left back once," she said.

"Hi," I said and put my hand out to shake his. He ignored it and said, "I'm hungry," and entered the house.

"This is Janet, she's a sophomore in college and has a boyfriend," said Jo.

"Hi," I shook her hand.

"This is Adrian," said Jo. "She's a mute."

"Ah," I said and shook her hand.

"No I am not," said Adrian. "I just don't talk much."

"Ah, ah," I said.

"This is my pride and joy, Margie, who is a senior in high school and is getting a scholarship to C.W. Post College next year."

"Oh, congratulations," I said and shook her hand.

"I wish Perry, that idiot, would learn from her," screamed Mrs. Mantroni so Perry could hear her no matter where he was in the house.

"And this is my husband and the father of my children, Gary," said Jo.

"Hi, Gary," I said and shook his hand.

"Thanks for inviting us over," he said.

His handshake was crushing. What is wrong with men who feel the need to squeeze your hand so hard that you want to moan in agony?

"We're looking forward to a nice evening," I said. *And after this Lucille and I are going to stick pins in our eyes because that's fun too!*

We sat in the living room.

"Would anyone like something to drink?" asked Lucille.

"We are a non-alcoholic family," said Jo solemnly.

"I'll have a beer," said Gary.

"Me too," said Janet. She defiantly looked at her mother. "I'm twenty one."

"That's two beers," I said and started to get up to go to the kitchen.

"No, no," said Lucille, leaping from her seat. I never saw her move so fast before. "I'll get them." She sprinted to the kitchen.

Silence.

"When's dinner?" asked Perry.

"What delicious thing has Lucille prepared for us?" asked Jo.

"Pizza," I said.

Silence.

"I had pizza last night," said Janet.

"That's because you don't like to eat healthy at home," said Jo. Then she turned to me, "I was under the impression, Frank, that Lucille was making a big home-made dinner for all of us to welcome you to our neighborhood."

Lucille entered with the two beers.

"Lucille," said Jo. "You said you were going to make a big home-made dinner for our family. But you are just serving pizza."

"I haven't got the pots or dishes unpacked yet," said Lucille, quite calmly.

"You've been here four days already," said Jo.

"Is the pizza warm?" I asked.

"I'm reheating one of the pies then I'll reheat the other," said Lucille.

"Well, here's to shit in your eyes," said Gary Mantroni holding up his glass of beer and then swigging half of it down in one gulp.

Janet raised her glass.

"None of us have anything to drink," said Jo.

"Soda? Water?" I asked.

"Coke," said Perry.

"Seven Up," said Adrian.

"Water with two ice cubes," said Margie.

"Do you have any scotch? I will occasionally drink in social occasions," explained Jo.

"Until she pukes it all up," said Perry.

"Uh, we don't have any scotch or any hard liquor. We don't drink that stuff," I said.

"And what about guests who do?" asked Jo.

"None of our friends drink hard liquor," said Lucille.

"And you don't consider us friends now?" asked Jo.

"Uh, ah," I said.

"Ah, uh," Lucille said.

"They don't even know us yet for Christ's sake," said Gary. "Shit in the eye!" and he swigged the remainder of his beer.

A half hour later we were eating pizza. Gary had eight beers in that half hour. Jo had five beers.

"This pizza sucks," said Perry, working on his third slice. "Where'd you get it?"

"Antonio's," said Lucille. "They were the only ones who would deliver."

"The pepperoni tastes like someone's butt hole," said Perry.

"What?" I said.

"Perry, sthut yo fuckin mouf!" yelled Gary Mantroni. He swigged the last of his ninth beer, "Pie tit!" he said holding out his bottle for us to give him another one.

"What did I say?" asked Perry.

"He's an animal," said Janet to Lucille confidentially at the top of her lungs.

"At least I'm not giving hand jobs," said Perry eating the butt-holes off the pizza slice.

"Tha's enuff of thaths," said Jo. "Ness thyme we com we geth a home-laid meal."

"I think I have to go and study," said Margie. She left.

"My boyfriend is coming to pick me up," said Janet. She left.

"I'm outta here," said Adrian. "I don't want to miss my shows."

"I'm gone," said Perry, grabbing another slice as he got up to exit.

Silence.

Gary was bleary. So was Jo.

Silence.

"Would anyone like me to warm up the fourth pie?" asked Lucille.

"Noah," said Jo.

"Buuuuuurp!" said Gary.

"Well, I guess that's it then," I said standing up.

"Canth ah hae thas pied?" asked Jo. "Fo lunsh?"

Gary was staggering towards the door. Lucille went into the kitchen and brought out the fourth pie to give to Jo but Jo had already gone out the front door now too.

Lucille closed the front door. She came into the living room; put the pie down on the coffee table.

We looked at each other.

"I will never allow them to ever come over here again," she said.

"Maybe we could ask them to move," I said.

At 2AM I woke up to . . . silence.

"Are you awake?" I asked Lucille.

"Yes," she said.

"There's nothing going on," I said.

"Thank God," she said.

And shortly we both fell back to sleep.

We learned that the Mantroni mid-night fights were intermittent. You could actually go three or four nights before the next bomb-blast occurred. After awhile we actually got used to it and I even slept through some of them. Gregory slept through them from the very beginning and when our second son Michael was born he never gave an ear to the Mantronies. I guess you can get used to anything.

The only permanent damage the Mantronies caused us had to do with the slight slip of land we had on their side of our house. It was maybe five feet wide, right next to their driveway.

Gary Mantroni was always fixing old beat-up cars and there was a lot of spilled oil on his driveway blacktop. So he'd sweep it onto my dirt on the side of my house. I wanted to say he swept it onto our grass but nothing could survive all that oil. That side of our house was all dirt—all greasy dirt. I never bothered to tell Gary to keep his oil to himself. He might have shot me.

I lived there for 10 years until Lucille and I separated and eventually divorced.

During those years, Jo Mantroni was a major figure in the church despite the fact that every organization she took over found itself losing members in droves. Janet got pregnant by some guy who fit right into the Mantroni yelling machine. Margie got that scholarship and I never saw her come home again. Adrian moved to live with her lesbian lover. Perry continued to live with his parents, helping his father in his business, whatever that was.

I did learn a very valuable lesson living in Valley Stream those years, the most important of which was—never move next to a house that has a sign saying how happy everyone living there is.

Happy Home . . . Oh, by the way, I never did meet that institutionalized one. I always thought of him as the lucky one.

17

Boys Will Be Boys

Bless me father for I have sinned. I gave bad example.

[Argument with my wife here:
"You really aren't thinking of publishing this are you?" asked my wife.

"I am," I said.

"It is disgusting," she said.

"I think it is funny and heartfelt," I said.

"It is disgusting and not funny," she said.

"It is funny," I said.

"Women are not going to like this chapter," she said. "What guys find funny women do not find funny. This is a guy chapter—and disgusting."

"When the women read this chapter they will have already bought the book," I said.

"What about the editor at the publishing company? What if she is a woman?"

"I am publishing this chapter," I said. "Giving bad example is a sin in the Catholic Church."

"Writing a disgusting chapter is a sin against writing," she said.

"We just disagree on this, that's all," I said.

"I am right and you are wrong," she said. "You are just being stubborn."

"Look, A.P., you had me get rid of six other chapters . . ."

"They did not fit the theme of the book," she said.

"The other chapters are gone," I nodded. *"But this one stays."*

She shook her head, *"I will divorce you if you publish this chapter."* She walked away.

I really don't think she'll divorce me over this chapter.]

[**Wife:** *I just might.*]

I have two wonderful sons. The oldest, Gregory, is a fine professional editor and a terrific writer with two beautiful children, John Charles and Danielle. My youngest one, Michael, is a chemistry teacher and world traveler. I have a great relationship with these two kids, I mean, these two *men*. I love them and just as important, I respect them.

Trite as this might sound, God where did all that time go? My little boys whose little bodies I would hug and whose soft little-boy faces I would kiss are now accomplished grown men. Both of them are far smarter than I and that isn't just my bias speaking.

But they weren't always men. As every parent knows it is an interesting, sometimes terrorizing, ultimately enjoyable trip from childhood to adulthood. It isn't a leap, even though in retrospect life seems to have jumped from back then to right now.

I remember little Greg asking me hundreds of questions about this, that or the other thing and then hanging on my every answer. Dad knew everything when Greg was little. Now I ask him questions and I hang on his words. Greg always wanted to be a writer, and he wrote short stories and his lead character was always named John, the name he gave to his son.

I saw my little Mike once put my belt around his waist—three times around because it was so big compared to his little waist. Mike asked me a question here or there, now or then, but he always seemed to know everything anyway with little help from me. He still seems to know everything without the arrogance associated with knowing everything.

Little Mike used to take mechanical things apart, such as a clock radio, and put them back together again—leaving out many parts that had been in it, "Dad, these things aren't needed," he'd tell me.

And the damn radio would work perfectly and there, scattered on the floor, would be all these unneeded parts.

Even as I write this I have a picture sitting right here in front of me on my desk of my two men as little kids, and I also have a picture of all the "Scoblete boys" as we call ourselves, taken some years ago: my late father John Scoblete, me, Greg, Mike and my grandson little John Charles, at that time only eight weeks old—yes, the Scoblete boys.

Greg and Mike formed an interesting contrast from childhood through college. Greg was always laid back as a teenager and young adult, and my wife, the Beautiful A.P. and I were convinced that if a statue were ever erected for him it would have a remote control in its hand. Talk about a Type-B personality! On one trip we took to Vegas, we gave Greg, who was staying at home, a $100 bill for an emergency. As soon as A.P. and I left the house, he cashed the $100 bill by buying $25 worth of cigars which he and my brother-in-law smoked on the porch each night we were away.

On the other hand, Mike was far more intense as a kid; a hard worker; totally alert in school—he rarely had to do homework because as he said, "I am an active listener. I pay attention in class and never daydream. School is work, not a time to play around." When we gave Mike that $100 bill for an emergency, he still had it when we returned home. Greg had cigar stains.

As adults, Mike has become far more intense if that is possible, an active world traveler, a builder for Habitat for Humanity and a gifted chemistry teacher. Greg has become a complete Type-A personality, working seven days a week on his writing deadlines and blog. No more cigars for him!

Still, my little Greg did have his ways.

Greg must have been seven years old, a cute little guy with curly blonde hair—bubbly, vivacious, and one Saturday morning I heard a crowd of little kids outside the house under my bedroom window. It was about 9 o'clock.

"Can Greg come out!" some of them shouted.

I went to the window and there had to be about 15 kids outside, all about Greg's age. Who knew my little guy had so many friends?

"Yeah, I'll get him," I said.

"He said he'd take us to the candy store," said one little girl.

"The candy store?" I asked. Why couldn't they go to the candy store without Greg, it was just around the corner?

"He said he'd take us," said another voice out of the crowd.

Greg made his appearance. All the little kids cheered and he led them down the block and around the corner to the candy store.

About 20 minutes later Greg and a few of the kids came back to our house and Greg waved goodbye to them and these few kids went merrily on their way gobbling bars of candy into their chocolate smeared mouths.

The next Saturday the same thing happened.

When Greg returned home I asked him, "Why do the kids need you to take them around the corner to the candy store?"

Greg was silent.

"Don't they know how to get there?" I asked.

"Yes," he said.

"So why do they need you to bring them?"

"I buy them the candy," he said.

"You *buy* them the candy?"

"Yes," he said.

"How do you buy them the candy?"

"From the money I find," he said.

"You find money?" I asked.

"Yes," he said.

"Do you have money now?"

"In my room," he said.

"Show it to me."

We walked up the stairs to his room. Inside he opened a drawer, took out a shoe box and handed it to me. Inside was change and also one-dollar bills, five-dollar bills, 10-dollar bills and even a few 20-dollar bills. How did this kid get all this money?

"You found all this money?" I asked.

"Yes," he said.

"All at once?"

"No," he said.

"Where did you find all this money?"

"In pockets," he said.

"In pockets? What do you mean in pockets?"

"In pockets," he said.

"Which pockets? Where?"

"When you leave your pants on the chair in the bedroom, I find the money in the pockets," he said.

"My pockets? The pockets of *my* pants?" I asked.

"I use the money to treat the kids to candy and ice cream and toys sometimes," he said.

"Greg, Greg, that's my money," I said.

"But I found it," he said. "It was in the pockets."

"Greg," I said. "That is called stealing. You took something that didn't belong to you."

"But it was in the pockets," he said.

"Those are *my* pockets," I explained.

"The pants weren't on you," he said.

"That doesn't matter," I said.

He just looked at me with a quizzical expression on his face. "It was treasure," he said.

"Greg," I said. "If I came into your room and took your *Star Wars* figures when you weren't there, am I taking treasure or something that belongs to you?"

He was silent, thinking. "Something that belongs to me," he finally said.

"And when you go into *my* pants pockets are you finding treasure or are you taking something that belongs to me?"

"You," he whispered.

"Me," I said. "Do you remember how many Saturdays you have been treating all the kids in the neighborhood to the candy store?"

"Four," he said.

"Four?"

"Maybe five," he said.

I looked at him again.

"Six or seven," he finally admitted.

"What you did was called stealing," I said. "Taking something that doesn't belong to you is wrong. We don't steal."

"But the kids all liked me," he said.

"They liked that you treated them. Real friends, you won't have to treat them for them to like you. They will like you because they like you."

He had tears in his eyes now.

"I am not going to punish you but you must promise me that you will never take anything that doesn't belong to you."

"I won't," he said.

As far as I know he never "found treasure" again and he was still able to have plenty of friends.

[**Wife:** *"That part is cute and taught a good moral lesson. But what has it got to do with you being a wayward Catholic?"* **Me:** *"Jeez, I am just showing the underlying framework of our personalities."*]

My wife Lucille and I were in the midst of trench warfare when our boys were six and three years old. Our marriage was a ship on the shoals, a slowly sinking wreck of a battleship. At this point, we looked for ways to irritate each other on a daily basis, before the actual bombardment of a full-blown divorce took place. Lucille would read books where the husband was brutally murdered by the wife and I would come home from teaching to see her nodding her head and looking at me as if to say, "What happened in this book could happen to you."

To counteract this mental murder maneuver, I taught my kids to help me torture her—even though those poor innocents didn't know they were part of my master plan. When I came home from work I would yell out, "Mister!" as loud as I could and Greg and Mike would come running to me from wherever they were, simultaneously shouting at the top of their lungs, "Wonderful!" (Yes, *Mister Wonderful*—that was me!) Then I would hug them and maybe give them a treat. This drove Lucille crazy.

My booming voice: *"Mister!"*

Their little voices: *"Wonderful!"*

During this delightfully vicious time between Lucille and me, I had been asked to describe marriage and I said, "Marriage is two combatants in the same bed."

During my six-year divorce ordeal from Lucille, I moved out of the house and I lived in two apartments—the first at Grove Street in Lynbrook, New York. I took my kids just about every weekend and let them help me with the plays my theatre company performed. In my tiny apartment we all slept in what I called "the Big Bed," Mike on one side of me; Greg on the other side of me. Greg was a peaceful sleeper. You wouldn't know he was there unless you opened your eyes and saw him breathing rhythmically.

Mike, on the other hand, was a wild beast when asleep; tossing, turning, kicking, moving his body so it fell all over you; twisting, tumbling. I woke up in the morning sore as could be from Mike's night moves. In fact, after a month of this Greg and I nicknamed Mike "Moving Mooch." It got so bad that I finally had to bring in another bed and cram it into the small bedroom. No one could sleep with the devastating "Moving Mooch" in those days without fear of dismemberment and death.

[*My wife the Beautiful A.P. hates when I talk about the following subject—and I think this is what got me into trouble with this chapter. She thinks discussing this shows no class; no culture; no sense of decency, no intelligence and that I should not delight in discussing it or, even worse, performing it or triply worse, writing about it. To her the whole topic is disgusting—to say the least. God knows what she will say when she reads this. But I can't help myself. I love . . .*
Farts!]

[**Wife:** *"I am telling you, your women readers are going to find another writer to read. Going through with this next section is a bad idea. Stop being so stubborn. You want to talk about 'wayward' then this whole chapter is wayward. You are warned."*]

I am a delighter in my own farts—as most men are delighters in theirs too. Indeed, women have no idea of just how gross and disgusting we men can be. Men delight in the disgusting. In fact, many of us revert to walking on all fours when women are absent. Only a man could invent the whoopee-cushion, rubber poop and fake vomit. But no doubt farts have the highest station in our hierarchy. My Lord, as children we actually practiced fart noises on our hands and arms—wet ones, dry ones, loud ones, squishy ones. You'd be hard pressed to find any girl who would do a thing like that! In fact, a few weeks ago I went to the T-Ball game of my grandson John Charles and after the game all the little boys were sitting in a circle blowing farts on their arms and laughing like mad.

Truth be told, Greg, Mike and I championed each others' farts for many years. We'd sit in the living room after dinner, reading our books and first Greg and then I would start cutting them.

"Woe! That was a good one, Dad," said Greg.

"Yeah, Gregster, nice one!" I said to him.

But Mike was the champion of our household. It took him some time to get warmed up after dinner—his farts had to percolate some—but then he would rip them mercilessly, and boy did they stink! When his "hot ones," as he called them, rocketed out, he'd wave his hand to scatter the odor. "Wait till this one hits you!" His boomers were tremendously loud as well. Greg and I were in awe of Mike's gastro-atomic talent.

Ba-boom!

"Oh, ho! Man!" yelled Greg.

Ba-boom! With a hand wave.

"Whew, man, that one stunk!" I'd say.

Ba-boom!

"Mike's on a roll!" Greg laughed.

Ca-ba-ba-booooom!

"Jesus, the atomic bomb!" I delighted.

"You guys are disgusting," A.P. would say.

[**Wife:** *You are still disgusting.*]

"Don't listen," I'd say. "This is men stuff."

"You are animals," she'd say.

As good as Mike was in loudness and nauseating stench, he wasn't the extended family's leader in *consecutive* farts. My cousin Bobby Quattrocchi was the best in that category. Bobby could cut consecutive farts like no other human being on the planet. I think he rivaled the great apes of the steamy dark jungles of Africa in this. Of course, Bobby was the generation before Mike, but our family records transcend time and place. Like baseball, farts are eternal.

Bobby was and still is the *consecutive* farting legend.

The rule for consecutive farts was simple; a fart counted if it was cut within 10 seconds of the previous fart. If it took 11 seconds, the consecutive streak was over.

My extended family on my mother's side shared a "country home" (actually a bungalow) in Sound Beach on Long Island, New York, and we would spend the summers there—the women, Aunt Mary, Aunt Tess and Aunt Annie, and the children, Eileen, Paulie, Michael, Margaret, Maria, Phillip, Emil, Frankie, my sister Susan, me and the redoubtable Bobby spent all summer in Sound Beach, while the husbands, Uncle Phil, Uncle Nicky, Uncle Rocco, along with my father and mother joined everyone on weekends. There were three bedrooms; one for the women and girls; one for the men and boys; and one for Nana Rose, who slept with a nightcap on her head and whose snores in the night sounded like Godzilla's roars. She was so old fashioned she even kept a chamber pot in her room. I am not sure if she ever used it.

During the week when the fathers weren't there, the male cousins all tried to rip those farts in succession after we were put to bed. Phillip, Paulie, Michael, Emil, Frankie and I all tried to get those consecutive farts to last until Armageddon. The best any of us could do was 38 in a row. That was Bobby. But others had consecutive farts in the 20s so Bobby's record seemed capable of being broken.

The best I ever did was 16. I was the worst at the consecutive farts contests.

From the girls wing we could hear the laughter as the boys oohed and ah'd at those farts. So the consecutive farting contest had a pretty big audience.

Then *THE NIGHT TO REMEMBER* arrived.

Bobby had discovered if he drank several bottles of soda his farting prowess became almost uncanny during his afternoon practice sessions. Many people don't realize this but to become a champion farter takes daily practice. It's a skill that requires discipline and diligence just like any other skill.

Opening the contest that night, Bobby's brother Phillip ripped an amazing 40 farts in a row to break Bobby's previous record. All the boys cheered. What an event!

"Shut up, up there!" yelled Aunt Tess from downstairs. Aunt Tess was unanimously acknowledged as the best yeller of all the aunts and she was Phillip and Bobby's mother.

Now it was Bobby's turn as all the cousins had done their best but none could match Phillip.

Bobby had snuck up several bottles of Pepsi to the men's bedroom. Bobby guzzled them while the other cousins were vainly trying to beat Phillip. Bobby had an interesting farting technique too. He'd pump air up his anus when he felt he was running out of gas. This air stimulated his expulsatory capabilities.

Bobby now got on all fours, pumped some air into his rectum and his monumental streak started. He passed Phillip's 40 with no problem and we all cheered when he hit 41.

"Hooray!"

The girls were giggling in the girls' bedroom too.

"Shut up, up there!" shouted Aunt Tess.

Bobby's farts were now exploding furiously. He didn't have to start pumping any more air into his butt until fart number 80. We boys were in a state of ecstasy as Bobby started pumping hard.

"Come on, Bobby, keep blasting," cried out his brother Phillip, not the least bit jealous that his own short-lived record had been shattered by his baby brother only moments after he had established it.

"We are witnessing history!" I shouted.

"A world record," said Paulie.

"Will you boys shut up or I am coming up and killing all of you!" screamed Aunt Tess.

We now started to chant the farts: 85! 86! 87! 88! and Bobby was now wildly pumping air into his butt but unfortunately those farts started to lose their power at 89, 90, 91, 92.

I could see Bobby's face too. He was sweating profusely. How much longer could this young dynamo continue his world shattering fart feat?

"Come on Bobby, get to a hundred," cheered Michael.

Could he? 93! 94! 95! 96! 97! 98! The time between 97 and 98 was nine seconds. Bobby pumped in air like a mad man.

Time ticked by.

"Come on!"

"Come on Bobby!"

"Go, go, go!"

Three seconds left.

"Bobby! Bobby! Bobby!" we chanted.

The tenth second came . . . and went. Bobby made it to 98—the all-time record for consecutive farts, a record never matched even to this day (as far as I know). We boys cheered like maniacs and then Aunt Tess catapulted her bulk into the room thinking she could surprise us.

But we had too much practice with her. We could hear her slinking up the stairs. She was too heavy to creep up the stairs quietly. Those stairs creaked like crazy. In a split second we were all silent and pretending to be innocently asleep. Phillip even pretended to snore.

Aunt Tess looked around the room, trying to see whom she could catch pretending to be asleep. No one moved. We were experts in feigned sleeping.

"This room smells awful," said Aunt Tess as she left.

[**Wife:** "Scobe, you have just lost your female readership."]

Greg and Mike were different in many ways. I had a little game I used to play with them in the car called "The Dancing Spider." I'd make my hand form a spider and have it dance up and down and around on the middle armrest and whichever son sat next to me in front got to play with the dancing spider.

I even sang a song about it: *The dancing spider! The dancing spider! The dancing spider! See the dancing spider! He's a friend to me and you!* And my hand-spider would dance around.

Greg would make his own dancing spider that would dance with mine, or he'd pet my dancing spider. Greg was a peaceful little kid. Mike, on the other hand, would kill my dancing spider by slamming his fist down on it. My dancing spider had to really zip out of his fist's way or it would get flattened.

If Mike flattened it, I'd let out a dying spider scream in a high-pitched voice, "The dancing spider is dying," I'd moan, and my spider would wiggle and slowly die. A few moments later I'd have the dancing spider come back to life and I'd sing again: *The dancing spider! The dancing spider! The dancing spider! See the dancing spider!*

He's a friend to me and you! And Mike would try to kill the dancing spider again.

As a father I had supreme magical powers too. When we came to a red light I could wave my hand, say "Presto!" and have the light change from red to green. That wasn't hard to do because I could look at the light for the other traffic, see when the yellow light came on and know that in a second or two, my light would turn green. The kids delighted in this magical display by the all-powerful mystic dad. As most fathers know, lying to kids is great fun.

Where I was really awesome, spectacular; where I hit my ultimate peak of godliness for my two sons, came when I *created* the snow.

"Tomorrow, my boys," I'd say in a mysterious, somber voice, "my magic sense tells me that it will snow all over our area. I can feel it. I will create the snow for you. When you wake up in the morning you will see snow covering all the ground. I have decided to bring the snow so you can have fun playing outside and making a snowman."

The boys would run to Lucille, who by this time knew I had no magic at all in anything I did (meaning *anything*), and she'd roll her eyes as they said happily, "Daddy's bringing the snow! Daddy's bringing the snow!"

I was right every time, too, thanks to the National Weather Service.

Finally on one of my mystic snow-bringing evenings, as I exerted my awesome magical powers over the weather, I told my sons to look for snow in the morning, and they ran joyfully to their mother, crying out "Daddy's bringing the snow! Daddy's bringing the snow!"

Lucille, by this time totally appalled by my awesome weather creating powers, said to the boys, "Yeah, well, tell Daddy not to create snow on the driveway or on the car."

I loved to play games with the kids because I loved to watch them win. Unlike some fathers who seem to enjoy crushing the little egos of their sons by beating them at various games, I went to the opposite extreme. When we played Monopoly I would forget to buy properties on which I landed by acting distracted. My sons would roll the dice fast so I could never buy Boardwalk or Park Place. They amassed fortunes at the game, while poor Dad stayed *poor dad*. I had actually thought of writing a book titled *Poor Dad, Poor Dad*.

But playing poker with Mike was the most fun. I dealt him hands that only occurred once every billion years! This kid got more royal straight flushes and more hands of four aces than anybody in history. He came to expect outlandish hands on every deal.

To make it more fun, I would deal myself great hands too. I'd have four kings; he'd have four aces. I was living with the Beautiful A.P. in my second apartment in Oceanside, New York at this time and when I got a good hand I would whisper loudly to her, "I've got four kings; I'm going to crush Mike, ha! ha!" She'd respond, "I feel sorry for Mike now, the poor kid."

Mike could barely contain his glee, knowing his four aces could beat my four kings. His little face would light up and he'd bet all his money as he kept raising me. I'd caution him against stupid betting. "You know Mike; I could have a great hand and win all your money." He'd nod trying to suppress a huge smile and continue to raise my raises until the pot was bulging with pennies.

Then I would lay down my cards with a flourish—"Four kings sucker!"—and reach in to take the pot and Mike would flip over his cards—"Four aces sucker!"—I'd bug my eyes out. "How did you do that? How could you get those aces? I can't believe it! My four kings lose."

Mike would haul in his cash thinking that the gods of chance really smiled on him.

There existed only one fly in Mike's miraculous ointment. Sometimes A.P. played and she would want to deal. Unfortunately for the gambling Scoblete boys, A.P. doesn't know how to cheat and so she dealt her cards legitimately. That meant Mike didn't always win when she dealt. He told me in confidence, "I don't like the way A.P. deals. She doesn't give me good hands. I think she's cheating."

[**Wife:** "Okay, some of this is cute and might show bad example but many readers never made it past the fart section. They may just have put the book down never to open it again."]

18

My Mass

Bless me father for I have sinned. I am a wayward Catholic.

The Beautiful A.P. and I go to Sunday Mass at 7:30 in the morning. I enjoy the Mass per se because I get a subtle feeling that I am participating in something that is centuries old—even if it isn't since the Mass is now said in English, not Latin, and the altar faces the congregation and the lay men and women are allowed to now touch the Host giving out Communion and, Heaven forbid, so are those who are receiving the body and blood of our Lord Jesus Christ. I mean today I am allowed to touch the Host!

I do feel bad for all those priests over all those centuries that had to root out the tiny pieces of wafer from the vomit of history's Mary Louise Roncallos. They are probably in Heaven annoyed at God for such an injustice.

I'm over 65; the Beautiful A.P. is over 55. We are the youngest people in the church! At this Mass we are the children. The rest of the church is filled with the coughing, sneezing, choking, yawning, gurgling, farting, drooling, slumped-over elderly—in truth the 7:30 Mass sounds like a tubercular ward. You have to hope that God is protecting the two of us from the hundreds of *them* and the billions of their germs.

A.P. and I sit right up front to the left of the altar (if you face the altar) and even though part of our view is cut off by the lectern, we like these seats. A.P. likes them because she feels closer to God.

I like them because it is the furthest distance between me and the bubonic plague carriers in the rest of the church.

At the lectern during Mass a lector will read pages of scripture from the Old and New Testaments. The first and fifth weekend of the month I am a lector at this Mass. So far I have not been hit by lightning.

The lectors take monthly turns at the various Masses (I also get an extra if there is a fifth weekend in a month). At 7:30am Mass we have a sweet woman of about 50 who does a good job—you actually understand what she is reading. We also have a psychotic guy who used to stand on 42nd Street in Manhattan screaming out his condemnations of the world (he has since been medicated).

And then we have Mr. Mumbles.

Mr. Mumbles is the worst reader of all time—Satan can read the bible better. This guy doesn't speak; he mumbles into the microphone. Here is an example of today's reading: "This is mumble, mumble, mumble John mumble, mumble God mumble, mumble, mumble, mumble Jesus, mumble, mumble, mumble . . . ."

When the priest was giving his homily this morning Mr. Mumbles, who is older than a giant redwood, fell asleep! There he was, sitting right behind the priest, Father Donovan, who was giving his usual great homily, and Mumbles' head was bobbing over his lap, his eyes closed shut, with drool coming out of his mouth, and to make matters worse, he was snoring! You could hear him all over the church in between the coughs and gurgles of the other elderly parishioners.

As Father Donovan finished his homily, we all stood up. As some of you non-Catholics know, the Catholic Mass has all sorts of standing, sitting and kneeling moments. This standing woke Mr. Mumbles who looked around and realized he wasn't dead yet. For the rest of the Mass, Mumbles went in and out of sleep states. Even standing he started dozing off.

At the very end of the Mass he had to tell everyone what events were occurring this week at the church. "This week—mumble, mumble, mumble, divine, mumble, mumble, mumble . . . ."

Thankfully, I only see him once a month and being a good Catholic I can sort of tolerate this pain in my ears. Actually I can't . . . I fidget and fret and A.P. has to (gently) kick me to get me to relax.

So having been tormented by the early morning lectors I decided to offer my services. I am an excellent reader having had over 33 years of teaching English and over 12 years in the theatre and numerous television appearances and radio interviews and . . . okay, that's not humble but it is still the truth. What the heck, if I were going to attend Mass I might as well enjoy it. So I became a lector. I even have a little fan club but it is getting smaller as the older women in the club keep dying. That's the kind of crowd the 7:30 Mass attracts. Many of the folks at this Mass can go directly to their own wakes when the service finishes.

One Easter the psychotic and I were to be the lectors. Each of us was given a role. I was given the starring role; he was a supporting actor with few lines. The head of the lecturing division of our church knew who should read what.

But when we got there the psychotic said, "I am reading the big part." His eyes were twirling in his head.

"I think I've been given that part," I said.

"I am reading that part," he said, his eyes twirling in his head.

No use talking to him. I turned to the priest, the ancient Father Wymes, "Uh, Father, I think I am reading that part."

The psychotic's eyes were twirling in his head. Was that foam I saw on the side of his mouth?

Father Wymes, who had served in Africa for most of his adult life and was now retired and living in our parish, looked at the eyes twirling in the psychotic's head and said, "You two can work that out."

So the psychotic got to read the big part and to be honest—he stunk up the joint. He has this weird voice—a voice that screams out, "I am insane!" He would take huge pauses between or actually in sentences. These were not dramatic pauses to enforce the reading, they were just pauses. Once I stepped on one of his lines because I thought he had gone into a fugue state but he turned his head to me and gave me a murderous look. "Sorry," I whispered.

I will never lector with that maniac again.

Now there is this woman who is always trying to come to church early enough to take our seats. Can't this creature see that these are *our* seats in church? I mean we beat her to the seats almost every Sunday but she won't give up.

We used to arrive at 7:30 Mass at about 7:25, but then *she* started to be there in our seats. So we came at 7:20; then she started to get there earlier. We are now arriving at 6:55 and the doors to the church aren't even unlocked at that time.

"Aren't you acting a little infantile?" asked A.P. when I told her we had to get there just as the church swung open its doors.

"No," I said. "*She* is forcing me into this."

Thankfully this woman is really old and even if she is there at the very opening of the church doors, we can beat her hands down because she can't move too fast with that walker of hers.

My God! As a Catholic she should well know the teachings of Jesus Christ to turn the other cheek and let me have the pew I want. Not to be cruel but she should take her two "other" cheeks to some other row and not try to plop them down in our pew. This is *our* Mass and we like *our* seats. Why is she so selfish? When she dies she will have to answer for this sin.

Seriously, I would never *wish* her to die but if she did, like this week or tomorrow or in about five minutes, I would sincerely hope she makes it to heaven. I really do. But I can tell you if she does, Jesus better watch his own seat. He'll be sitting *second* to the right hand of the Father.

Finally, God's subtle sense of torture also sends me the "garlic couple," a husband and wife who eat so much garlic that they would be able to kill Dracula.

I have a very sensitive sense of smell. When I was a child my father said to me, "Your nose is a curse, Frankie. It will hurt your entire life. Mark my words." He was right.

I am nauseated by the "garlic couple" when they sit behind me which they often do. They breathe that stench at me and it is a *day-after* stench, garlic roiling around in their lungs and bloodstream, mixed with bad morning breath. It could kill. I sometimes actually feel a Mary Louise Roncallo moment coming on for me.

So for most of the Mass, with them behind me, I try to hold my breath as long as I can without breathing in. This causes me to have an altered state of consciousness where I swear I see visions after awhile, one of which is drowning the "garlic couple" in 50 gallons of Listerine.

Then there is my mortal enemy—Last Word Man—who sits midway in the church. But when I am the lector I can see him. Oh, yeah, mister Last Word Man, I can see you.

The Beautiful A.P. and I would often go for an early morning walk and on these walks I ran into my greatest opponent, my greatest antagonist; the man I am going to defeat if it takes me ten billion years! *The Last Word Man!*

We meet this guy at various stages of our walk. He always seems to be out there waiting for me. He's always in church behind me and I am sure, even without looking, that he is smiling at the back of my head.

A.P. and I say hello to him and he says hello back. This is feigned friendliness on my part. I am promulgating a lie of friendliness because I am incensed that he always has to get in the last word, *always*.

Here's how it goes:

ME: Good morning.
HIM: Good morning, how are you?
ME: Great. Thanks.

Now A.P. and I walk on. I mean the guy is now 10 or 20 feet behind us. With a normal person that is that. But no; not him.

HIM: Good, good, good.

He got the last word in! He *always* gets the last word in.

This has been going on now for over 20 years and I am sick of it. So I have decided . . . *I have sworn an oath as I sit in front of the garlic couple* . . . to not let him get the last word in; to somehow, some way, one day, just one stinking day, to be the one to get that last word in.

Yesterday and today were the first days I tried to defeat him. Here is a word for word description of what happened.

ME: Good morning.
HIM: Good morning, how are you?
ME: Great. Thanks.
HIM: Good, good, good.
ME: Good.
HIM: Yup.
ME: Good, good.
HIM: It's a beautiful day.

He's now at least 20 feet past me but I have turned around so I can make sure he hears me.

ME: Yes, wonderful.
HIM: Yup.
ME: Yup, yup.
HIM: Enjoy yourself.
ME: Thanks.

We are now about 50 feet apart.

HIM (*shouting*): Take care.
ME (*shouting*): You too.
HIM (*shouting*): I will.
ME (*shouting*): I will thanks.
HIM (*shouting*): Thank you.
ME (*shouting*): Thank you too.
HIM (*shouting*): Take care.

He turned the corner just then and I had to stop shouting because if anyone saw me they would have thought me shouting to no one and added me as another village idiot to the several we already have. I know he knew just how close to the corner he was so he timed his "take care" for just the right split second.

One day we met him coming into the Post Office. I turned to A.P. and whispered, "I am going to whip his ass today." She replied, "Don't be a baby." I replied to her reply, "His ass is mine."

ME: Good morning.
HIM: Good morning.
ME: Great day.
HIM: Might rain later.
ME: Yeah, might.

A.P. was getting the mail from our Post Office box where our business mail is delivered. Our box is down near the floor. My nemesis was just mailing a letter. So I knew the conversation wouldn't end here but he had to leave the Post Office, right? My plan was to get the last word in as he was leaving, closing the door behind him. I bent down to A.P. and whispered, "Take your time; I want him to leave first."

A.P. rolled her eyes.

HIM: My grass can use some rain.
ME: And you could use some grass, ha! ha!
HIM: Huh?
Obviously this guy has no sense of humor.
ME: I was joking, ha! ha!
HIM: Oh.

He was now walking to the door. A.P. was starting to get up. "Stay down, stay down," I whispered to her. "This is childish," she whispered back.

"Just stay down, will you?" I begged.

"I'll count to ten and that is it," she said.

ME: It's kind of early; maybe I'm not so funny.
HIM: Well, get home before the rain.
ME: You too.
HIM: Thanks.
ME: Yup.
He was now opening the door. I knew I had him now.

HIM (*almost out*): Yep.
ME: Yup.
HIM (*door starting to close behind him*): Yep.
ME (*almost triumphantly*): Yup.
HIM (the door is only two inches from closing fully): Yep.

I have this bastard now! I would get my "yup" in and the door would close and I would turn my back to him and I WILL WIN!

HIM and ME (simultaneously): Yep/yup.

And as the door closed, with lightning speed he said another "yep" which got into the lobby with the door ajar maybe one-millionth of an inch and then the door was closed completely and he walked away fast—again the damn winner.

"Can I get up now?" asked A.P.

Of course, Last Word Man had to be a Catholic and he was one of those types of Catholics who was so damn holy in church, so damn serious, that no one knew what a bastard he was. But I knew. Oh, sure he said the prayers really loud so every stinking, coughing, sneezing, wheezing, drooling plague carrier could hear him. His prayers were always just a touch late so his was the last voice you would hear.

When I was the lector I could see him making the sign of the cross and praying. But he couldn't fool me. I knew the truth. I knew the damn truth about him. And someday in some way I will get the last word in. I could see me strangling him, "Go ahead, go ahead, try to speak, I dare you, try to speak."

Other than these small hassles, going to Mass is comforting.

19

Books

Bless me father for I have sinned. I am a coward.

Thirty years ago I had over 5,000 books in my private library. I was an avid reader to say the least and I had read just about every book I had. I looked at those books and believed that each and every one of them was now lodged in my brain, making me more aware, making me smarter, making me, well, *me*—even though, frankly, I could barely remember what the hell any of them were about.

Then I went through a divorce from my first wife Lucille and she took about a thousand of those books, mostly the costly ones, or the ones that were collector's items. That was fine; lose some good books, lose a bad marriage—fair deal.

A couple of years ago, my Beautiful A.P.—a *librarian* no less!—decided to get rid of most of my books. For a few years now she has been throwing out one book a day. It took me a couple of years to realize that my collection had been whittled down about 20 percent since A.P. was intelligent enough (no, make that devious enough) to go after books that were on the ends of shelves or piled high on top of the book cases.

But I did finally notice.

"Are you throwing my books out?" I asked.

"I'm following your mother's advice," she said.

"What?"

"Your mother told me that in order to have a neat house you can't have stuff cluttering up the place," said A.P.

"My books aren't cluttering up the place. They are the road map of my intellectual life," I countered.

"Come here," she said. "Take a look at these books."

She held up a ratty old paperback I had bought as a kid that when opened fell apart the way ancient texts would.

"Do you really think you can read a book like that again?" she asked.

I mumbled something incoherent, as I always do when the Beautiful A.P. has me nailed against the wall, and she said, "There are hundreds of paperbacks like that and hundreds of rotten hard covers. You're never going to read all these books a second time. Get rid of them."

"Let me explain," I stammered. She gave me that look that says, "Explain what?"

"Okay, okay, I'll compromise," I said. In marriage "compromise" to the man means the husband lets the wife have her way if she just gives him a teeny-tiny victory in some little, miniscule, worthless area. What compromise means to the wife is different—"I will wait to get my complete way eventually." Compromise to a woman is just delayed total all-out victory.

"You can throw out the ratty paperbacks, okay? But no hard covers. And no quality paperbacks that aren't falling apart. No philosophy books; no science books." I said.

"What about science books that are so old the science has changed? You have science books here that say the Earth is flat," she said.

"Okay, throw those out too," I conceded. "But no books on religion. No bibles . . ."

"You have a dozen bibles," she countered.

"All different translations," I said. "And no Korans; and no Jewish mysticism books or any books on any religion."

"Okay," she said. I had held her off a little for a little while.

So the giant purge began and when all was said and all was done, I had about 1,500 books left.

"My book shelves look so bare," I said.

"You keep space on book shelves to make them pleasing to the eyes," she said.

"My eyes were pleased to see all those books," I said.

"I wasn't pleased to see all that dust," she said.

There wasn't much dust on the shelves any more.

That was 10 years ago. Since I don't take books out of the library, even though A.P. is a librarian, I slowly started building my collection up again. I was down to reading about a book every week or every two weeks, unlike the ferocious pace I had set as a kid and as a young man. In those days I read every spare moment I had. But I could still see those new books beginning to come back on my dustless shelves.

Then yesterday, *just yesterday*, A.P. stood in the dining room, then in the living room, then in my office and then in our storage room and said, "We have way too many books in this house. I want to get rid of half of them."

"What? What? Half? No way. No way," I said firmly in my most mannish voice. If I were in the military and I used that voice I could get our side to nuclear bomb Starbucks.

"We still have about two thousand books, including those dusty collections of old books . . ."

"They are collector's items," I said firmly.

"No they aren't," she said. "Your collections of series don't have all the books in the series."

"What difference does that make?"

"No one buys a collection if the collection is not complete and if you look at yours, not a single one is complete. And they are also all falling apart."

"My beauty, my beauty, I'm keeping these authors alive," I said as if I were a doctor saving someone's life during open-heart surgery. "Most of them are obscure writers. They live on my shelves; otherwise they don't exist anymore."

She gave me *that* look. All husbands know *that* look. "Alright, alright," I said. "Just those collections; nothing more."

"You have all those Stephen King books, all the horror books, hundreds of gambling books, and all those old science fiction books you read as a kid. Tell me you have to keep Stephen King alive. Do you have to keep Edgar Rice Burroughs alive?"

"I was a young adult when I read those Burroughs books. It's my past," I whined, an inch from agreeing to compromise—meaning an inch from total defeat.

"And you still have ratty paperbacks and old plays you used to do when you acted. You have about a hundred plays that are falling apart. And . . ."

"Okay, okay," I said, totally defeated. In married life when husbands and wives have it out, if the husband loves the wife with all his heart and soul, as I do the Beautiful A.P., then we let the wives win. Why? Because if we keep fighting day after day, week after week, year after year—we're going to lose anyway! So what's the point? Give in and be done with it.

If you really want to know how to have a great marriage follow this advice: The very first sentence you should say to your wife in the morning is "I'm sorry dear." And the second sentence you should say is "You were right dear." That should cover you for the day.

A.P. could see it in my face—total 100 percent defeat about these books at the hands of a far more powerful opponent.

"I want to clear room on the shelves for pictures of the family. Of our beautiful grandchildren," she said triumphantly.

"Fine, fine," I whispered. "But I get to pick the books."

"Yes, but I want 500 gone," she said. "Maybe a thousand."

There was no arguing with her now. She was striding through the house like Cleopatra having just killed Mark Antony with an asp.

I started to go through the shelves. At first it wasn't really that hard. All the old paperbacks that remained from the last purge fell apart when I took them off the shelves. I took all the old "Science Fiction Book Club" novels and made a pile of those. In them were all the planets, all the future civilizations I had visited as a kid.

Some of my old texts and books from my masters' degrees went. I had a collection of almost everything on Ernest Hemingway—a collection that was, I'll admit, almost as old as Hemingway would be right now—in fact, that collection looked kind of like Hemingway looks right now. F. Scott Fitzgerald fell apart as well. D.H. Lawrence, Charles Dickens, a whole collection of Shakespeare's plays just crumbled when I touched them. Quality paperback books on poets and other great writers withered away when I removed them from the shelves.

Then I grabbed a book *Plain and Simple: One Woman's Journey to the Amish* by Sue Bender and threw it to the floor.

"What are you doing?" asked A.P., who was closely supervising me.

"What do you mean? I'm getting rid of books," I said.

"That's my book," she said pointing to *Plain and Simple: One Woman's Journey to the Amish* by Sue Bender.

"So?"

"We're keeping that book," she said.

"It's falling apart," I said.

"We're keeping that book," she said. She handed me the book and I put it back on the shelf, after blowing a mound of dust off it. I whispered to myself, "Damn thing looks like it's been on an Amish farm."

Shortly after, I threw another book to the floor. "That one doesn't go out," said A.P.

"It's so old you can barely read the print on the back," I said.

"That's Harpo Marx's autobiography. That's one of my favorite books," she said.

"Look, you read library books, you don't read real books," I said.

"Real books?

"You know, I mean books you buy and own," I said. "We don't need this crap in our library, do we?" I asked.

"That book stays," she said.

I opened the book. "My God, there are bugs crawling around in this."

She gave me *that* look.

"I'm serious," I said vowing inside myself to fight this battle to the death. I held the book in front of her face but she refused to look close enough to see these little bugs crawling around in it. Several pages crumbled like dry leaves in the winter.

"Put the book back," she said.

I looked at her. I thought of my vow to fight this battle to the death and . . . I put the book back. We compromised by throwing out 500 of my books and none of her books.

20

Koala

Bless me father for I have sinned. My teaching almost caused a murder.

I was a great teacher. Yes, I was. The following is just one example that proves my point.

There was this student Koala, a hulking baldheaded kid who used to scrawl his name all over the walls of the school with arrows going through it—constantly getting suspended for doing that. Maybe he loved himself. A lot. Being suspended didn't faze him one bit either. He may have set the all-time record for suspensions for a kid *not* thrown out of school. He was a tough son-of-a-bitch too.

But I must say Koala and I had a great relationship. I liked him. He liked me.

I used to have my students—no matter their intelligence level or their behavior patterns or whatever else the educational system labeled them as being—memorize many poems and many excerpts from Shakespeare's plays.

They did it too. The regents (academic) classes, honors classes and advanced placement students memorized the poetry because they were hungry for high grades. I didn't have to finesse them very much. This was an easy 100 just for doing a little work. But not all my students were hungry for high grades; especially my "S" level students (non-academic) who had to be cajoled in various ways.

I would say that Mike Tyson (or whoever was considered tough at the time) would crap in his pants if he had to memorize poetry. Anyone can fight. The biggest idiot in this class can fight. Then I would name a kid as the biggest idiot and everyone would laugh. I would also tell them that when they were standing on the street corners or in the alley ways or in the 7-Eleven parking lots, smoking their joints, wouldn't it be fun to recite these poems to their friends? Wouldn't their friends be impressed by them? That was good for a laugh too.

And on we went with the memorizing. In 33 years, I never had a student not do it—which in itself was a hell of a success.

Koala loved memorizing the poems. He'd strut into class, bald head agleam, muscles bulging, and he always wanted to be the first one to recite. He was good too. He put in expression and passion and his favorite author was the man himself, William Shakespeare. He set the bar in memorization that the other students had to reach for.

And that is why he is in prison now for attempted murder.

You see, Koala was arrested for attempting to rob a bank using a shot gun to scare the tellers into giving him money. This was the day after he graduated from high school. They gave him a few thousand but the money was rigged to explode into a red cloud and the cops followed Koala's cloud and nailed him.

He went to a state prison for armed robbery.

One early evening Koala was reciting poems on the dinner line. "'Tomorrow and tomorrow and tomorrow / Creeps in this petty pace from day to day' . . . ."

"Shut the fuck up," said another prisoner.

"This is Shakespeare," said Koala.

"Shut the fuck up," said the other prisoner.

"'To the last syllable of recorded time' . . ."

"I told you to shut the fuck up," said the other prisoner.

Koala punched the guy in the mouth with all his might and several of the guy's teeth went flying down his throat. The guy started choking and coughing up blood. Koala jumped on top of him and pounded the guy's head into the floor. When the guards restrained him, the other prisoner was out cold, blood streaming all over the floor from the wounds on his head and in his mouth, and Koala was madly reciting the rest of the Shakespearean quote.

The other guy didn't die. No one ever told Koala to stop reciting his poetry after that. Koala now serves 25 years for attempted murder.

It's great to be able to reach your students, isn't it? I felt this was one of the highlights of my career even though it almost cost someone his life. As a teacher you take what you can get.

"And all our yesterdays have lighted fools the way to dusty death."

21

Steven Spielberg

Bless me father for I have sinned. I bore "true" witness against a priest.

I never met him. But I met some people who knew him.

I was called to Hollywood to discuss a movie script I had written that never got made taken from a novel I had written which hasn't even been sent to a publisher yet.

I met with six representatives of the movie company this day.

My script had been sent in by my former agent (may he rest in peace . . . even though he isn't dead) to the movie company's reader, who liked it; who then sent it on to someone above her in the company who liked it; and on up the long, long ladder until a full producer read it, liked it, and set up the meeting with me to discuss it.

I took the very first flight to Los Angeles from Kennedy Airport in New York, high from excitement that I might get my first movie script produced. I had been told over the phone that my script "knocked us out!"

A limo picked me up at the Los Angeles airport (I thought: "Oh, I'm gonna be rich! I'm gonna be rich!" to paraphrase Ralph Kramden from the *Honeymooners*) and on we went to the big Hollywood office where the meeting would take place. Movie scripts often sell for more than a million dollars. ("I'm gonna be rich!")

The six producers sat around a large oval table and in control of the meeting was the oldest producer in the room—a boy of about 24, whom I will call the Ancient-One. Some of the movie folks around that table looked as if they just finished toilet training. One could have . . . *I swear to God* . . . been a fetus. None dressed in business clothes—as I had because the Beautiful A.P. had said, "You want to make a good impression. No sweats like you usually wear." Hollywood is a dressed down industry. Remember that if you ever go to a meeting such as this.

"Mr. Sco-bleet-tea is that how you pronounce it?" asked the Ancient-One.

"Close," I said. "Sco . . ."

"Why don't we just call you Frank?" asked a Sour-Faced girl with tattoos all over and rings in her ears, nose, mouth and tongue.

"Fine, fine," I said. "That's fine with . . ."

"Good, Frank, let's get to this because we are very busy," said a Red-Faced boy.

"Let me say," said a Pimply-Faced boy. "I loved the script. It was so different. Not like any of the scripts and concepts we usually get." Then he picked one of his pimples.

"Unique," said Red-Face.

"Yes," said the Ancient-One. "Your murder weapon blew my mind too! Wow! Wow!"

"It was so dark but I laughed my tits off too," said a Bright-Faced girl who looked about 11 years old.

"Well, they are big enough," stated Red-Face.

"How much did they cost?" asked Sour-Face.

"Your script Frank has the makings of a very funny but intense movie," said the Ancient-One.

"Great," I said, adjusting my tie. I never wear ties. I have one, the one I wore, and I wore it to make that good impression the Beautiful A.P. told me to make. I should have just worn my normal sweat suit. I would still have been the best-dressed person in the room.

"Let's get right down to it," said Red-Face. I nodded.

"We keep the murder weapon," said the Ancient-One. I nodded.

"I think we need them to fuck," said Sour-Face. The others around the table nodded in agreement.

"Fucking is very important," said Bright-Face.

"What?" I asked.

"Within ten pages," said Pimply-Face, still picking on that one—*big*—pimple on his chin.

"Ah, uh, this is a story of unrequited love," I said. "The tension in the movie comes from that; you know nothing is happening but emotionally underneath it's building, that's the idea."

"It can build after they fuck," said Sour-Face, not even looking at me but looking at the others. "We can show that in coming attractions to attract the boys in the audience who want to see tits and ass."

"Now do you think we can make Angela a man? You know Angelo or something?" asked Bright-Face. "That might give it a different twist—push that envelope—gay on straight sex leading to murder, pretty good. Maybe they have sex together when Bobby gets high so he is willing to let his inner gay man out of the closet but it doesn't work out."

"Well, she has a husband," I said. "I mean without the husband, the whole murder thing . . ."

"Not bad, not bad," said the Ancient-One to Bright-Face. "Kind of like the *Crying Game*."

"No, no," said Red-Face. "You'll turn off the teenage boys. They don't want to see two guys blowing each other. *Brokeback Mountain* bombed in the Red States."

"They're all idiots," scoffed Sour-Face. The entire table exploded with laughter.

"I wasn't thinking of any sex scenes between Bobby and Angela at all," I said. "It's *unrequited* love."

"To have a successful movie, Frank, you have to have selling points to sell it," said Pimply-Face.

"But I thought you all thought the script was unique?" I asked.

"Yes, but we have to add things that the audience likes," said Sour-Face. "The audiences aren't as smart as us."

All of them nodded.

"So we pump in a really furious sex scene right from the start," concluded the Ancient-One. "Get the movie off with a big bang." Everyone at the table laughed.

"Uh, just a second, you see, ah, the idea behind unrequited love here is that she is creating all sorts of romantic scenarios with him in it as her lover but he is actually repulsed by her," I said. "Their business relationship goes down the tubes because of that, leading to what we think is a murder by him but . . . ."

The others looked at me with uncomprehending faces. I stopped talking for a moment.

"You do know what *unrequited* love is?" I asked. I mean these were children; maybe they had never heard of the idea of unrequited love.

"Explain it," said Pimply-Face evidencing boredom and picking at some scabs now.

"There's no return on it," I said. "It's not returned. Your love is not returned by the person you love. It hurts you to the core of your being. That's what this movie is about. That's what sets everything in motion here. Love hath no fury like a woman scorned."

"What's that got to do with sex?" asked Bright-Face.

"This movie will be R-rated right?" asked Sour-Face.

"I imagine," I said. "Yes, I think so."

"R-rated with no sex?" asked Sour-Face. "Come on."

"No, no, there is a sex scene around page sixty but not with Bobby and Angela but with her stoned out of her mind and . . ."

"Blowing a stupid dwarf stage hand? There's no sexual tension there," said Red-Face.

"He's not a dwarf," I said.

"He's short. Dwarf, short, what's the difference?" said the scab-picking Pimply-Face.

"Bad boy," laughed Bright-Face. "But I like the idea of the stage hand being a dwarf. What do you say, should we make him a dwarf?"

"You don't even see her head bobbing up and down in the damn scene," said Sour-Face. "Bobby walks in at the end of it all. You don't even see the dwarf tense up to come."

"There *is* tension," I said. "The tension is between Bobby and Angela when he walks in on her having sex. Angela thinks she is making Bobby jealous as opposed to nauseated."

"No, no," said Red-Face. "We have a gorgeous actor playing Bobby and no one sees him in the buff? Will that create word-of-mouth among the young girls? No. We need to see his tight ass."

"I still like the gay idea," said Pimply-Face.

"Television is pushing the envelope like crazy today," said Bright-Face.

"Isn't there one coming up where someone drinks a whole glass of piss?" asked Sour-Face.

"I heard the drinker likes it too," said Pimply-Face. "That's a true breakthrough."

"We need that kind of radical thing that television is doing in your script, Frank, my man" said the Ancient One. "Make it unique. Push that envelope."

"The murder is unique and never thought of before," I said.

"Yeah, but we learn the truth at the end," said Red-Face.

"What envelope breaking things do we get *throughout* the movie?" asked Bright-Face.

"I think there is tremendous humor and horror in recounting their relationship," I said.

"You have to understand that people today have a very short attention span," said the Ancient-One fiddling with his pen.

"Some of your scenes last more than a page," said Pimply-Face.

"We have to cut them down or the audience will doze off," said Red-Face.

"The theatre scenes are funny," I said.

"Yeah but most of the movie audience has never been to live theatre," said Pimply-Face dabbing some blood from one of his pimples with a tissue.

"Except maybe their high school plays," said Sour-Face.

"Which stink to be honest," said the Ancient-One. "So let's see. In a rewrite we want to get them into bed within five pages. Let's establish the concept of murder right then . . ."

"Wait a minute," I said. "You know she is murdered on the very first page."

"Yeah, yeah, that has to come out of the script, really. Why give the whole plot away right from the first line?" said the Ancient-One.

"What?" I asked. "Don't give it away on page one but give it away on page five?"

They ignored me.

"I still think we need a gay presence in the script," said Bright-Face.

"Let's really push this on the R-rating," said Sour-Face. "We should have them banging away throughout the movie but Angela loves Bobby but he doesn't love her; he's just using her for his own selfish satisfaction; a typical man."

"He's not a typical man," I said. "He's different. Both of these characters are different and that's what gives the script its power. Bobby is a truly different type of man."

"Because he is really gay!" shouted Bright-Face. "You see we push the envelope on love."

"Interesting, interesting," said the Ancient-One. "Okay, Frank, the script needs heavy revisions. Go with our recommendations. We all have experience."

I looked around the table. Experience? In what? Chewing on pacifiers? These children had never lived life. They were products of television. Their real world was the television world they grew up with.

The Ancient-One continued, "Being a new screenplay writer we aren't going to sign a contract with you until we see you push that envelope a bit."

Push the envelope? Push *what* envelope? Having someone drink piss? What kind of envelope was that? Here's a real envelope pusher for you: Why not a weekly television series on a major network on William Shakespeare's plays? Prime time too! That's pushing an envelope—not piss going down someone's throat!

"Let's forget this script for a moment," I said. "Let me pass an idea to you that might push that envelope of yours to the extreme."

"Sure," said the Ancient-One.

"I had a teacher in high school known as Father Conga. He was a priest, and the reason we called him Father Conga is because he had a bullet head sunk deep into his massive shoulders and his jet black hair while short was really, really curly. He looked like an ape. He had long arms and he walked like an ape too.

"He'd always talk about how we had forgotten the Old Testament God who would be the one to judge and punish us—and we were all going to be punished he promised. While saying this stuff about the Old Testament God he would dig all the way into his huge flat nose and take out snot and make it into balls which he lined up on his podium and then he would shoot them off into the class as he talked about the punishment of the Lord.

"The students had to duck and go side to side to miss getting hit. But every once in awhile one of us would get a big wade of rolled up sticky snot on us—sometimes on our glasses or in our hair. The best way to avoid this was to sit in the front and we'd all run in after lunch to get to those front seats since his snot balls usually went up in a 45 degree angle.

"How do you like that as an idea for a movie? We can call it *Father Conga: Snot Man from Hell!* That really pushes the envelope doesn't it?"

The children at the table looked at me, considering.

"That might make an interesting television show," nodded Bright-Face. "Add a lot of funny characters, snot flying around in each episode. That might really work."

"Bring that to our television division," said the Ancient-One. "It's got great potential."

The door flew open. An old, old man of about 36 entered the room. He glared over the boys and girls and, holding up my script, he said, "I can't sell this shit to major movie chains. It's an Art House film. We pass on this shit. There's no money here."

He was the marketing director, the real boss of all bosses, and he had passed judgment on my "unique" script. It was—to push the envelope—"shit."

I flew back to New York three hours later. I took a taxi to the airport. Un-paraphrasing Ralph Kramden, "I'm *not* gonna be rich! I'm *not* gonna be rich!"

I never bothered to write *Father Conga: Snot Man from Hell!* even though it would be helping to push television's envelope.

22

The Wedding of the Century Or Evangelical Christians versus the Kosher Caterer!

Bless me father for I have sinned. I am guilty of harsh judgment.

My wonderful niece Melanie is getting married next Sunday. Her father-in-law is the minister of her church, a fundamentalist Christian church where the services last so long they prove the existence of infinity.

Okay, fundamentalist religion is her thing, fine, good, if that is what she wants. I am hoping she outgrows it and returns to the more relaxed confines of the Catholic Church but I have no say in this.

My niece's side of the reception is composed of Italians; many "just off the boat" as they say, some of whom speak little or no English and if someone dies the women wear black for the rest of their mortal days and light candles in the local church. Her side also numbers American Italians and mixtures such as me (Irish, German and Italian) and the Beautiful A.P., my sons, grandchildren and cousins.

The groom's side of the reception will have mostly Italians "not just off the boat" and many various blazing-eyed pastors and ministers from various fundamentalist Christian churches. Some marriages don't have a prayer; this one will have hundreds!

The reception is being held at—*hold your breath*—a kosher caterer! No mixed milk and meat and probably that horrifying coffee-mate with your coffee. I don't even know if the men and women will be allowed to dance together.

The Italians just off the boat have no idea of the kosher world. Their table should be interesting to watch during the festivities.

Where the real thunder and lightning comes in will be with all those fundamentalist pastors, ministers and followers. They like to pray—a lot. No meal goes by without a long, loving tribute to Jesus (the food gets cold) and then there are all the hallelujahs and even some speaking in tongues. All that should go over big in a kosher place.

Now we will be able to tell whose side God is on. If lightning comes out of the sky, striking dead those pastors and ministers and followers jabbering in tongues, I am converting to Judaism. If nothing happens, I'll stay where I am, comfortable in my wayward Catholic mindset, thank you. I will also continue to eat dairy and meat.

The day before my niece's wedding I had a 24 hour bug that made me go great guns to the bathroom every few minutes. I thought I might have to miss the wedding on Sunday, March 13. No such luck. Keep in mind this was the wedding of Christian fundamentalists where the reception was being held at a kosher caterer. The new "chosen people" versus the old "chosen people." Could be—literally—a blast.

But other miserable things have happened to me since I wrote the first part of this chapter. My dash board went out the day before the wedding and now needs more than a thousand dollars in repairs and also the Beautiful A.P.'s multi-billion dollar watch stopped working. So things were not going well.

Keep in mind this wedding ceremony was packed with evangelical Christians of the extreme variety. My cousin Michael, an actor, wanted to know if they were bringing poisonous snakes to bite all of us in order to test our faith. Sadly no one spoke in tongues or flailed around on the floor foaming at the mouth but there were dozens of ministers present and most were of the slick television variety that you usually see down South on television condemning every damn thing except condemnation. They wore expensive suits, colorful ties, big diamond rings; they had perfectly coiffed hair—you get the picture.

The groom's minister father (named *Damian*, no less) is slick and friendly and he did the ceremony. He was very good. He has a strong stage (or is that altar?) presence although his script was overlong by about an hour or two.

The church was being rented and it was a beautiful church. Reverend Damian did not have his own church; he rented a senior citizen center. I asked one of the guys who worked at the rented church what denomination it was. "What do you mean?" he asked.

"Is this a Lutheran, Anglican, Methodist church?"

"I don't know," he said and wandered off.

Then the custodian came by—I assumed he was the custodian because he was dressed in blue work clothes and looked a little unkempt, he was also sweating like crazy too—and I asked him the same question.

"Denomination? The church? Who the hell knows?" he said and wiped his nose on the back of his hand.

The ceremony was long (loooooonnnng); a lot of bible passages about the wife being subservient to the husband. I kept nudging the Beautiful A.P. when those "obedience" passages were read. A.P. had removed the word "obey" from the "love, honor and obey" portion of our wedding ceremony and substituted "cherish." She hasn't obeyed me once in over two decades of marriage!

There was a second minister helping with the service. He looked like he came from "The Sopranos"—think of Luca Brasi from the "Godfather." A bruiser; tall, big boned, fat with a scary face. He had some scars on that scary face too. He definitely looked like the muscle of the Lord's outfit. He had no stage (altar) presence though. He muffed everything he had to say; fumbled and mumbled fifty million times. It was as if he had never done a wedding ceremony before. Maybe the only thing he was good at was breaking the knee caps of sinners.

During one point he went ballistic. He started howling, "Damian [the groom] you will forgive Melanie [the bride] and Melanie, you will forgive Damian!" Okay, said once, even with this minister's eyes bugging out, fine, okay, fine, let's move on and get this interminable wedding over with. But no, no; he kept going, "Damian you will forgive Melanie, and Melanie, you will forgive Damian! Damian you will forgive Melanie, and Melanie, you will forgive Damian!" Over and over and over. Some of the members of the congregation rhythmically moved their heads back and forth.

"They might be bringing out the snakes," said cousin Michael, the actor.

Finally the minister's strange episode receded and we moved on and finished the wedding. Actually, the wedding was not really bad; just a little nutty at times.

This wedding was packed too. There were around 250 people. We were not allowed to throw rice at the couple outside the church because rice kills the birds. A true New Yorker said, "They aren't birds; they're pigeons."

So we were given bubbles. When the couple came out, we were to blow bubbles at them. Unfortunately for us, it was a hell of a windy day and the bubbles kept blowing in everyone's face. The wind seemed to only blow *into* your face so if you turned around, you still got hit smack in the face with the damn bubbles.

A.P. said, "Maybe we should have been given bird seed to throw? That wouldn't kill the birds."

A woman said, "No, I went to a wedding where they did that and a bird shit right on the groom's head. The birds shit on all of us!"

So now it was the reception at the kosher caterer. The cocktail hour had so much food that we wouldn't need to eat a dinner. Everyone from the church started praying their individual prayers as they sat down with the cocktail-hour food. Jesus' name was mentioned a lot. I kept looking around to see if any of the Jewish waitresses were getting upset. (I knew they were Jewish because many had stars of David dangling from their necks.) I guess they were so busy they didn't hear anything.

The biggest question the Beautiful A.P. and I had concerned who the heck was that scary hit man who seconded the Reverend Damian at the wedding. When the groom's mother passed me, I got her attention.

"Marian, I was wondering who the assistant minister was helping your husband," I said. "The big guy."

"He's a prophet of the Lord," she said.

"A prophet; you mean someone who predicts the future," I said.

"He's always right," she said solemnly. I could see the big guy prophesizing. "I am going to break your legs, Bruno, with this baseball bat." Whack!

"Will he be prophesizing tonight?" I asked.

"No, he did so in church," she said and hustled off to the buffet.

Ah, so the assistant minister's wild "Damian you will forgive Melanie, and Melanie, you will forgive Damian!" was really a prophecy. I wonder what Damian and Melanie are going to do in the future that will require all that forgiveness.

The catering hall was quite nice. The service was excellent. Once the cocktail hour was over we all went to our assigned tables. A.P. and I sat with our son Greg and his wife Dawn, our grandchildren John Charles and Danielle (he was the ring bearer; she was the flower girl—two better looking and well-behaved kids you will never find at a wedding), our son Mike, the chemistry teacher, Charlie and Donna who are our daughter-in-law Dawn's parents; my nephew Jason and his effervescent girlfriend; and my brother-in-law Tony and my sister Susan, who is so thin you can't see her from the side. Susan and Tony were the bride's parents.

The usual stuff happened. The MC announced the wedding party, then "all hail" the bride and groom, and then the DJ played music that (as always) was so loud you couldn't hear yourself think, much less hear anyone at your table talk. When people did talk, you just smiled at them as if you heard them. ("My family was just killed by terrorists." Everyone around the table smiles.)

When the preliminaries were over, a big woman with dyed red hair got up to say the welcoming two-hundred-hour-long prayer. She disappointed me. She only said "Jesus," "Jesus Christ," "Our Savior," "Our Lord," "the Messiah," "God's son," "the second person of the Trinity" and the "one who will open the doors of heaven only for those who believe in him," about ten times each. (Okay, I exaggerate—five times each.) I checked the waitresses; they didn't even seem to notice.

Now as an aside, you will note that I do not make fun of Jews. I have two reasons for this. One, Jewish comedians make the best fun of Jews and, two; my friend Marilyn the Goddess would break my legs if I did. She is very sensitive. But I do have to say, nevertheless, there was great Chinese food at the cocktail hour. (Bahda bing!)

The reception was a major disappointment because everyone danced and had fun, just like they do at a regular wedding— well maybe this was just a regular wedding and my skepticism was completely unwarranted . . . except . . . .

I mentioned that we did have about twenty Italians, some just off the boat; some of whom might never have seen a Jew. One guy called over the waitress and in halting English said, "I want no margionae [margarine], I only eat butta [butter]." She politely explained that they didn't serve butter. He was confused but she smiled and walked away, thinking she had made a good explanation. Then the whole table chatted in Italian, with a lot of pointing, frowning and head shaking.

The wedding reception was long. It went from 5pm until 10:30. Truthfully there was a lot of money wasted on this wedding—money that probably could have been used as a down payment for a house.

The Beautiful A.P. and I danced with the grandchildren all night as they wanted to dance until I died.

And that is the wedding. You would think that would be that, but it wasn't.

Yesterday, the day after the wedding of the century, I had that damn diarrhea again. Then a giant cement truck drove by my house, caught the telephone wires way up there in the sky, brought them down along with part of the side of my house.

I didn't know it had happened, even though I felt the house shake. A policeman came to my door to tell me. "Your side has been ruined," he said. Cops don't show a lot of emotion, they are trained to be cool. He was cool. I, however, am not cool.

Immediately after the cop told me part of the side of my house had been ripped down I cursed, "Ah crap!" And then I had to go to the bathroom again. I closed the front door, thanking the officer as I did so, and ran to the bathroom.

Now I have a watch to fix, a dashboard to fix, my telephone lines and the side of my house to fix and I have to get back to normal bowel movements.

And I swear; I will never make fun of a religious wedding again. I will never exhibit harsh judgment. God is torturing me because I did. I apologize to all the evangelicals, other Christians, Mormons, Jews . . . and atheists . . . and anyone I've not specifically mentioned, okay? Just let everything get back to normal, God, that's all I ask.

23

How to Fix
the Catholic Church

Bless me father for I have sinned. The Catholic Church has really screwed up.

The Catholic Church is broken. American Catholics miss more Masses than they go to according to a private poll I took among my five friends. It is no longer a Hell-damning mortal sin if you don't go to Mass every Sunday. This annoys me as my fellow classmates and I feared going to Hell and getting squashed by THE BUS all those times I skipped out on Mass as a kid or lost some seeds on a daily basis except in the hours between confession on Saturday and Holy Communion on Sunday.

It has gotten ridiculous.

My sons went to a Catholic high school and the priests told them to "try" to get to Mass on Sunday. What is *that*? Try? Try! They had no fear of roasting for eternity? What has the Catholic Church become? I'd call that truly unfair to those of us who were damned based on almost everything we did. My sons could probably lose seeds all over the place with no fear of burning.

Actually, I agree with the new stance. It does seem pretty idiotic that some schlep missing Mass on Sunday has committed a mortal sin equal to the mortal sin committed by Dexter, the serial killer. So although the Church should be congratulated for growing up in this regard, it presents a dilemma.

Without mortal sin and Hell fire how are you going to get Catholics to come to Mass every Sunday or on Holy Days or any other time? Fear was the instrument the Church used in my youth and it sure did work. Our Lady of Angels Church was mobbed every Sunday and every Holy Day of Obligation. Now Mary Louise Roncallo could let lose one of her "comets" and not necessarily hit a parishioner. I say apply the God-given quality of logic, the logic God endowed us with, and use that to fix this particular problem. I have now done this and I can assure you my brilliant plan will get people to Mass.

Follow me closely now: the United States of America is unquestionably the fattest nation in the history of Planet Earth. We jiggle and jangle when our blubbery bodies trundle down the street. When we moon someone our asses are as big as the real moon. We love to eat. We live to eat. You won't find Weight Watchers franchises in Uganda but you need them in America. Interestingly enough, one of the biggest ways Weight Watchers makes money is by selling food! Those folks are not stupid.

So what does all this "fatitude" tell you? This: Why is the Church still giving out stale awful-tasting wafers as the "Host" at the sacrament of Holy Communion? I have never met a Catholic in my life who says, "Yummy, can I have seconds on that wafer?" The only reason Catholics eat the damn thing is because we believe it is the true body and blood of our Lord and Savior Jesus Christ. But come on, Christ tastes awful. You'd think the Son of Man and the Son of God and a guy who rose from the dead would be a little more flavorful. Jesus needs a top chef in that department if you ask me.

There is no law of nature or of the bible that states you have to give followers of Christ a tasteless wafer. Since that is the case, here is how to get more people to come to Mass. Change the Host from a tasteless wafer to a brownie. You'll see attendance skyrocket.

Give attendees a choice. They can have plain brownies or brownies with nuts. Then let them each get a glass of wine. Have you ever slurped down wine and chocolate? A wonderful taste combination! It is almost irresistible.

Think of this. All the blubberous fallen-away Catholics will crowd into church for some of those delicious brownies. The Church will get millions of converts from those dull Protestant sects in America alone. You can even advertise these brownies in Weight Watchers' magazines, "Come to the Catholic Church and eat a delicious Jesus!" And make those brownies big, not little crumbs. And make the wine a good vintage.

My word, those larger-than-life Catholics might attend multiple Masses on Sunday; in fact, they'll probably start coming during the week too. Think of the amount of money the Church can collect with all those extra-large bodies. Of course, you'd have to apportion the seating so that you have equal tonnage on both sides of the church or the building might list. But other than that it is a win-win situation. The Church gets more people to participate and the congregants become delighted with eating the chocolaty body and blood of our Lord Jesus Christ.

So that solves the problem of not getting enough people to attend Mass.

Next up the very idea of Hell and the afterlife.

Hell has always irritated me. Eternal fire? Other than excruciating pain what do you learn about your life other than that you screwed up big time? So let's take a look at Judgment Day:

"What did you do Adolf?"

"I slaughtered 11 million people, six million of them Jews."

"What did you do Mao?"

"I slaughtered 60 million people."

"And what did you do Frank?"

"I lost seeds in 1963."

But the old Church rules state that we are all in Hell because of the above sins. Now that is screwy.

My wife the Beautiful A.P. is now petitioning the Catholic Church to incorporate her brilliant concept of Hell by making it a "learning experience." She thinks that Hell has to be the ultimate lesson of what our actions have wrought.

"First we end the word Hell," she says. "Instead make the afterlife a place where every bad and good deed you have ever done is experienced by you from all the people those deeds, both good and bad, affected."

She has a great point. Take Adolf Hitler, the poster boy for evil in the modern world, and project his afterlife. He must experience the death of every person he ever killed. He now—one by one by one—becomes every Jew he slaughtered; every gay he killed; every Gypsy he extinguished, every mentally slow individual he allowed to be experimented on. Sounds pretty bad, right?

It gets worse.

Yes, when he is finished with all the above, he must now experience the effects of his actions on the relatives, friends, and people who read about his atrocities. Now that would be an afterlife of a different stripe—a far better stripe than the Hell of eternal fire. Experiencing your effects on all the people your life influenced will teach you something profound about your life. Certainly none of us would want such an afterlife that Hitler would have.

The Beautiful A.P. thinks everyone should go through this type of afterlife experience—you, me, the Pope, your nutty neighbor down the block, Mother Theresa, Genghis Khan, Bill Clinton. You will relive the effects of the good and the bad you have done.

It is a brilliant idea. Your life now becomes a learning lesson for you. I'm hoping that for someone such as yourself you won't have too many bad things to experience. Yes, calling Timmy Thomas "a bucktoothed bloated smelly farter whose mother is a hyena" might hurt you but hopefully experiencing the effects of doing such a nasty thing on Timmy's life won't take all of eternity unless, of course, Timmy is driven into becoming Ted Bundy.

Keep in mind you will also experience all the good that you have done. Your good deeds will indeed live after you.

So far no one in the Church's hierarchy has answered the Beautiful A.P.'s request to change their version of the afterlife but perhaps over time they will come around. The Church is slow to change its ways—after all, they just apologized to Galileo for not believing he was right. If the Church does not change the afterlife to A.P.'s way of thinking, may the hierarchy experience all the hurt they have caused my beautiful wife by their stubbornness.

Now, what about those recent miracles of Mary?

I hate to say this but Mary, the mother of God, has become a real annoyance. Yes, I know I should not be critical of a woman who remained a virgin all of her life (or is that completely nutty as many Protestants think?) and who was born without Original Sin unlike the rest of us saps. But seriously, except for Fatima and Lourdes which were almost a century ago, I am shamed to admit her latest miracles have been lame.

It seems that every day some devout Catholic lady, scrunching her rosary beads and muttering prayers in a wild-eyed way to a ham sandwich that resembles the Mother of God, or some strong muscled man pausing as he mows the lawn looking feverishly at a tree stump, that looks like the Queen of Peace or any of the people who are also seeing Mary in such tree stumps and ham sandwiches, in addition to leaf patterns, potato chips, branches, clothing, Swiss cheese, cheddar cheese, Cheese Whiz. Oh, and the lucky ones who get to see her statues crying—often crying *blood*—has happened so much that such a thing is becoming a public spectacle.

Seriously, what kind of image is this—a statue of the Mother of God bleeding (often from the eyes no less)—for a universal Church that is supposed to make us happy because we have been saved? Actually if this blood were real, analyze it and maybe it would make a good blood type for transfusions. "Oh, my, I feel so holy now after that transfusion. But I never want to have sex again."

We have a world continuously at war. Men and women and children killing men and women and children all over the planet all over time and Mary comes down and makes a potato chip look like her and then the intense Catholics pray to the potato chip. Nothing of any import actually happens. The world continues on its merry pace of destruction. No one even gets to eat the potato chip.

Couldn't her Son Jesus who is seated at the right hand of God (unless that woman from Mass has pushed Jesus into the second seat) tell her to do something a little more impressive than making a tree stump or mushroom in her own image? Maybe just stop one terrorist attack against school buses filled with children? Couldn't she appear at the UN and explain that if we continue fighting she is going to give us all a "time out"? How about a modern-day "loaves and fishes" miracle? Maybe she can even do a bigger one than her son did—maybe she could feed all the starving people in the world.

I really don't want the Holy Mother Church to associate itself with such shoddy Mary miracles. Is that so wrong of me? Let little cults have the potato chips and the mystical images in bologna sandwiches. Shouldn't Catholic priests explain to their parishioners that they should ignore all Mary images in such things as wheat bread and farina? I think so. Catholics should not be identified with lame supernaturalism. It makes us look stupid to scientific-type atheists who are now claiming much bigger miracles—such as the creation of the universe from nothing—meaning nothing as in "nothing"—without the need for God. Can you imagine? Catholics are seeing the supernatural in various food stuffs while scientists are uncovering the secrets of the universe. We are looking at tree bark and soy meal while they are looking at the very stuff of reality.

No tree stump, potato chip or bloody statue can stand up against profound scientific knowledge. The Church that's had its share of geniuses had better get its act together before Mary begins franchising her face like Colonel Sanders. Catholics should take note of this and keep their ham sandwiches and tree stumps to themselves.

Some church rules have hurt me personally. I mentioned in another chapter that I am a great reader but I am also a great speaker. I know, I know, I shouldn't write such things because it smacks of hubris but I have to write this in order for what I am about to say to make sense.

I may be a wayward Catholic but I know how to present material in a way that audiences find interesting and enjoyable.

[**Wife:** *"Do you have to be so blatantly egotistical?"*]

With A.P.'s blessing I looked into becoming a deacon in the Catholic Church a few years ago.

If you are an old-time Catholic that has fallen away from the Church or a Protestant who is trying to discover what our bunch is all about, a Catholic deacon is kind of like a priest. Think of him as a mini-priest or priest-light. Although he is allowed to be married when becoming a deacon, should his wife subsequently die when a tree branch that looks like Mary crushes her head in a freak accident, then he must stay single and celibate. He is able to assist at Mass and give homilies; he can perform Baptisms and he can work among the poor. Being true to Catholic traditions only men can become deacons.

The Beautiful A.P. and I went to the deacon meeting in our diocese of Rockville Center one evening. There were about 20 men there, some with their wives. Everyone was yabbering, mostly about what they did for a living and what called them to God. Since nothing but my ego was driving me, I basically listened and nodded sagely.

The head of the deacons in the area gave a talk about the glorious role the deacons play in the Church. He then said, "All of you should you become deacons are subject to the Bishop of Rockville Center and must pledge total allegiance, loyalty and obedience to him." Pledging total allegiance and loyalty and obedience to anything doesn't sit right with me. It seems to be a denial of my ability to make decisions.

Luckily I didn't have to worry about wrestling with that obedience dictum because the lead deacon then said, "If after the completion of the five years of training you would be sixty-three years old then you cannot become a deacon." Well, that was that. I would be over 63 when I became a deacon and so I was left out.

It is a silly rule. Instead of automatically eliminating me, why not give me an audition? Let me read a passage of the bible— even one selected at the last minute and therefore one I could not prepare for prior to my audition—and see what kind of homily I can come up with? Having seen so many deacons and priests stumbling, mumbling and giving lifeless homilies I am sure I could impress the judges. Put me in front of a few hundred people and see how I do.

Okay, okay, I was actually hurt (and a little angry as you can sense) that my age had eliminated me from being a deacon but shortly after that I had an even worse experience with Catholic procedures.

As you know, I am divorced. My first wife Lucille and I divorced in 1993, having been manacled together since November 2, 1968—a day that will truly live in infamy. We "separated" in 1986 but Lucille dragged out the divorce proceedings for all those years. If you know people who have gone through a divorce you know that it is always their "spouse" who was at fault. That "spouse" usually takes on the characteristics of Beelzebub—the horrendous demon looking to scar men's souls.

And so it was with my divorce. I was an innocent; she was the demon.

Lucille just wouldn't let me go and why should she? She wasn't working; I was supporting her, paying child support and sending her to graduate school. A perfect life—and I was out of her hair to boot. But then along came Fred, that wonderful guy from Texas, a true deity if there ever was one (he should have *his* face in a potato chip), riding in on a white horse and Lucille fell in love and finally agreed to the divorce. (I love you Fred!) She moved to Texas, married Fred who is a Baptist and (I assume) she is now living happily ever after. I even got the kids when she trotted off to the Lone Star State.

Okay, that's the framework for this other problem with the Catholic Church—a problem that needs to be fixed and fast—although it is too late for me.

I married the Beautiful A.P. within months of the divorce. Obviously we couldn't get married in the Catholic Church because the Church does not believe in divorce—it's another one of those mortal sins that can send you to Hell to suffer alongside Mao, Stalin, Hitler and Rock Hudson. But by 1993 I was in the "I'll decide what is and is not a true sin" and divorce certainly didn't fit into my continuum relegating me to eternal damnation.

Now the Beautiful A.P.'s mother was a stalwart in Malverne's Our Lady of Lourdes Catholic Church. She belonged to just about every organization (in the church and in the town) and was probably at one time or another president of each one of them. One year she was named "Woman of the Year" in Malverne, an honor she fully deserved each and every year. I have to say, I loved Peg; she was quite a wonderful woman.

Peg was Catholic through and through, and although she was happy that the Beautiful A.P. was happily married, she was sad that A.P. could not marry in the Church because of my divorce. However, the Catholic Church is a smart church and has a concept called "annulment" where the Church can declare a previous marriage null and void—making that previous marriage non-existent.

I always thought of this as a way to allow divorce while making some bucks on the side. It never appealed to me. But it did to Peg. After a decade and a half Peg asked that I get an annulment and marry the Beautiful A.P. at Our Lady of Lourdes Church. I agreed and set the paper work in motion.

It would take six months to a year. Okay, fine, it is always good to make your mother-in-law happy and truthfully it was no skin off my teeth. (That is some disgusting expression.) I needed to get affidavits from several people attesting to the fact that my marriage to Lucille could never have worked out and that it was therefore obvious that Lucille and I could not really have been married in the eyes of the Church—we were only married in the eyes of civil government and everyone else on Earth.

Lucille, now married to Fred, also received an affidavit. All she had to do was agree that we had no marriage and that would be that. I would be free to make my mother-in-law happy.

Unfortunately that *wasn't* that.

For some crazy reason—a reason never revealed to me—Lucille decided to challenge my getting an annulment of my marriage to her so that I might marry the Beautiful A.P. in a Catholic ceremony. Now I was told by the Church officials that the annulment—if it were to be granted—would take at least another year, if not more.

It dragged on . . . and on . . . and on—much as my divorce had from Lucille. Why she was challenging this I had no idea. I mean she had remarried someone who wasn't even Catholic. What did she get out of screwing around with my annulment? In fact, I hadn't seen her or communicated with her for years. And that has made me very happy.

Peg was diagnosed with cancer in January of 2009 and had one request of us—that I get that annulment before she died. I called the Church officials urging them to move fast but they told me there was nothing they could do to speed up the process because of Lucille's challenge.

Peg got sicker and sicker . . . and passed away on Wednesday, July 29, 2009—before the annulment came through. The day before Peg died I was sitting with her talking about books. I lied to her by saying that the annulment was a few weeks away and the Beautiful A.P. and I would be married the very day we got it. I was actually praying Peg would hang in there for however long it actually took although I wasn't even sure the annulment was anywhere near coming through.

Months after Peg died the Beautiful A.P. and I did marry in the Church. Evidently Lucille's challenge did not work against my annulment—her challenge merely delayed everything. At the ceremony A.P. and I had Annette and Dave as our matron of honor and our best man as they had been for our first wedding. No one else was invited or told about the wedding.

Father Frank, the Pastor of Our Lady of Lourdes, asked us why there weren't more people invited and the Beautiful A.P. told him, "We are doing this for ourselves. We have the people here we want." She meant not just Annette and Dave; she also meant the spirit of her mother. Peg was in that church that day to see her daughter get married properly. A.P. truly believed that. We toasted Peg at our dinner after the ceremony.

Divorce? Annulment? "A rose by any other name" and the Church should wake up to that fact.

Now let's take a look at some other traditions of the Catholic Church which should be changed tomorrow or the next day. Such changes would make the Church far more appealing than it is right now.

Priests should be allowed to marry. Maybe the idea of a celibate priesthood made some sense when it was first put forth, "Men, no more you-know-what with those wives. From this point on, no wives for you." I think it was the 13th (self-appointed) Apostle Paul (an unmarried guy prone to ecstatic visions, usually of Jesus) who decreed that it was better not to marry but if you were currently married not to do "it" because the second coming was on its way. Oh, sorry, he meant the Second Coming of Jesus—I mean in a spiritual way or, as conservative Protestants think, the Second Coming is when the Lamb of God, the man of peace and love, takes up a fiery sword and slaughters non-believers.

Although even a superficial reading of Church history would reveal that a lot of you-know-what was going on among celibate priests and young ladies / gentlemen in the various villages, towns and cities, the Church persisted in its guise of a celibate priesthood being the only type of priesthood. You would think the Church would realize that God didn't give us all those seeds to horde them.

What I am about to say is no knock on the thousands upon thousands of wonderful priests out there but, seriously, it is a little weird that anyone would go for celibacy. The Church's recruiting methods automatically eliminate all the guys who think, "I ain't giving up sex," and often appeal to someone who is not all that interested in rumpy-pumpy. Within the legion of the celibate are probably more—what should I call them?—maniacs than you would find in the legion of guys who wouldn't even think of giving up marriage (or giving up the mortal sin of losing seeds outside of marriage).

So dump the celibacy and allow married priests. They would add another dimension to the Church.

And allow women to become priests too. What's the big deal? I didn't see Christ going bananas because he had so many female followers. He seemed to enjoy the company of women. What is it that a priest actually does? He preaches the gospel and explains what God wants from us. He performs the sacraments of Baptism, Confirmation, and the Holy Eucharist (Holy Communion); he hears confessions, marries people, cares for the sick, the poor and gives the blessing before death for those who look as if they are about to kick the bucket. Why are these activities such that women are incapable of doing them?

Let's get cynical for a moment shall we? I think it is perfectly reasonable that the celibate hierarchy headed by the Pope, the cardinals, the bishops, the priests aided by traditional Catholics don't want anyone mucking around in their pool of power. Let married priests in and a semblance of normalcy will enter the Church; meaning all those damn women will have a powerful sway over their husbands to which all husbands can attest. Allow female priests and those annoying women will start to take over the Church and change other things as well.

The old guard is merely protecting itself from the possibility of an overwhelming new guard. The celibates will lose their power in the Church just as the Jews lost their power in the Church once the pagans joined Jesus en masse (mostly thanks to that visionary Paul). Married priests and women priests are the new pagans and once the Church's doors are opened to them, they will surely rush in and take over.

This next idea is really not going to sit well with even many liberal Catholics but here goes: Welcome gays into the Church by allowing them to marry in a Catholic ceremony.

Yikes! Isn't God convinced that gay acts are abominations? The bible said He said it, so I guess He meant it. But losing seeds as I did daily (sometimes twice daily, sometimes thrice daily) was a Hell-damning sin as well but no one told me I was not welcomed in the Church because of the delightful abomination in which I engaged. I was allowed to marry Lucille in the Church— and prior to that wedding I lost so many seeds in more than a decade that you could forest the Amazon fifty million times over. I was even ultimately allowed to marry the Beautiful A.P. in the Church although the Church's rules until that second Catholic wedding meant the Beautiful A.P. and I were committing mortal sins like crazy when we did you-know-what.

Let us say that the Church considers the act of you-know-what among gays to be abominations just like my seed spilling. Fine. But the Church also considers birth control to be a sin; it considers sex that doesn't end in the possibility of children to be a sin; it considers many things to be sins—in fact, the Church considers many things we do every day to be sins including some thoughts.

But won't allowing gays to marry in the Church and to be practicing Catholics encourage more people to become gay? Won't Catholicism get an influx of gays many of whom will want to redecorate the churches? (Please, no letters to me based on my stereotyping.)

Here is a rule that I love to follow. It is called my "I don't care" rule. I don't care if gays flock to the Church. I don't care if every Saturday there are gay weddings in Our Lady of Lourdes in Malverne. I don't care if some of my gay friends want to redecorate the church. I don't care. They can argue with the people who don't want to see the decorations changed. Have at it folks.

I don't care if you believe people choose to be gay or are born with some kind of gay gene (or DNA) that makes them gay. *I don't care.* Let science figure it out. Marrying gays is not condoning anything. I used birth control all through two marriages. If that's a sin then I will have to face God and shyly say, "I lost seeds even when I was wedded." God will then decide what to do with me. Important point, I was never kicked out of the Church for not having slews of children.

If a gay guy thinks he is committing sin by engaging in sex with his spouse, fine, go to confession and promise not to do that anymore. I used to promise that I would not lose any more seeds and you know where that wound up. I think God will be a lot more understanding of our human desires and actions than Father Sullivan. Gays would, of course, just have to worry about that damn BUS.

Jesus once said that before we try to take the small speck out of another's eye we should take care of the plank in our own eye. Makes sense to me.

Yes, all of us can be considered sinners. When asked what was the greatest commandment Jesus responded by saying, "Love God with your whole heart, mind and soul and love thy neighbor as thyself." Okay, based on that advice I am in sin just about all day every day. I rarely think, "Oh, I love God so much." In fact, unless I am writing about God or having some kind of conversation about God I am not pondering His greatness or effusing love to Him.

And what of my neighbors? You have got to be kidding! I have some neighbors I can't stand! I don't love them; I don't even like them. Yes, I know, I am violating Christ's recommendation and I am sorry for that but, please, there's a guy down the street that even Christ would have a hard time loving. And what about Last Word Man? I do not and never can love him. Even as I lector at Sunday Mass I look out over the congregation and there are people out there praying their hearts out that I really don't like. That's right in church no less—I don't like these people even when they are in church!

So if being gay is a sin is it any worse than me not loving God all day long and simultaneously disliking many of my neighbors even when they are in church? I don't see the Church throwing out all of the people who are just like me—totally oblivious of following those two simple rules laid out by Jesus Christ. My personal opinion is to stay out of people's bedrooms, let them live their lives, and if they have screwed up let them experience the afterlife as the Beautiful A.P. believes it should be.

The "I don't care" rule does not apply to everything, I'll grant you that. The civil authorities should hunt down criminals—even if the Church forgives those criminals their sins when they go to confession. Serial killers, murderers, thieves, muggers and people who don't use deodorant like the French must face the music. The "I don't care" rule does not apply to all things.

But welcoming gays into the Church by marrying them? I really don't care as long as none of them tries to take my seat at Sunday Mass! Then we have a problem.

24

Does God Exist?
Part One

Bless me father for I have sinned. I question the existence of God.

Does God exist? If He does exist, is He the god of the Jews, of the Catholics as I was taught long, long ago, or of the Protestants, of the Muslims or simply one, perhaps the most powerful one, of the innumerable polytheistic gods we've encountered in history? Is He the Hindu Absolute couched in the illusion of the world? Is He some alien from another planet, perhaps hiding in a mother ship above the earth as some recent religions believe?

Who knows? Do you know with absolute certainty? If you do, well then . . . God bless *you* because I'm all over the place on the issue.

Given a choice I prefer ancestor worship. I like the idea that my mother will look after me in her afterlife. I like it that Nana Rose will keep checking on me and that my deceased aunts, uncles and friends will keep me in their spiritual hearts and minds. Ancestor worship is the best of the best. You never really lose anyone.

In my opinion, Catholicism has a lot of ancestor worship. That's why at this stage in my life I like being a Catholic. I get to talk to the saints (the original connotation being those who are believers, not the recent view of those who did extraordinary religious feats during their lives—some of those saintly saints sound completely deranged) of my family and ask for their help . . . and continued love. In a way, Mary and Jesus feel as if they also belong to my family. God the Father? Not really. Way too removed for my tastes and really He is kind of—how can I say this delicately so I don't piss off my priestly friends?—off-the-wall in the Old Testament. The Holy Ghost (now called the Holy Spirit) as God? Come on, nothing to grasp onto; too nebulous.

Is any of this true? Is there a Trinity? Is Christ really that wafer I eat on Sunday? Was Mary a virgin her whole life? I don't know. And at this point in my life I really don't care. Believe what you want in these areas.

Let us say there is without question a supreme being, God, and He sees you have totally screwed up your belief system. You think Mary had 20 kids; you figured some of the Apostles were totally stupid; you think the Host is just a piece of bread, you think eating pork makes you holy. You think Christ was really disdainful of much of the Old Testament. You can go on and on about whatever mistakes God might see you making in your belief system. Now would the Supreme Being of Everything give a damn if you ate pork? Would He put you on a par with the great mass murderers of all time? How upsetting to Him can it be if you are a little stupid in the belief department? It doesn't upset me so why would it upset Him?

The question of God's existence is not really complex. In my 20s I was an avowed atheist. I could shoot down all the arguments for the existence of a god. No argument, be it design, ontological, or any of the other hundreds of ones could withstand my withering rationality. I was a brilliant young man if I do say so myself.

The bible certainly didn't help me form a positive opinion on God's existence either. Once I started reading the Old Testament thoroughly (something Catholics rarely do), the character of God can bug your eyes out. He is really a violent, infantile, silly, angry deity with a monstrous sense of self and with a strong aversion to pork and shellfish who loves the smell of burning mammalian sacrifices that give a "pleasing odor to the Lord." He loves battles and blood and punishments—Yahweh (that's the real name of the biblical God) is often a god of terror in the Old Testament.

And Yahweh—heaven forbid me—is really cruel when it comes to eating. For crying out loud why outlaw bacon and then make it taste so good? That is cruel and unusual punishment. Why make bacon and shell fish and fish without scales taste so good? That's nasty if you ask me.

Okay, putting aside things of my youth, and my harsh analyses, today I don't see Yahweh in this light. If the bible is a good book, as opposed to "The Good Book," then there has to be something more to it than Yahweh making the Pharaoh not release the Israelites (keep in mind that Yahweh "hardened the Pharaoh's heart" so that poor slob had no chance to let the Israelites go) and then killing all of the first Egyptian born and then all the Pharaoh's army after making a mess of the whole country with 10 plagues. Of course, if this event ever happened in real life, without an army Egypt would have ceased to exist. But that's archeology, not the story.

Is Yahweh the heartless being who punished all of mankind because Adam and Eve ate the fruit from the Tree of the Knowledge of Good and Evil? Did He drown the whole world in a flood, killing all the little babies who hadn't yet done any sinning unless soiling their diaper had become a crime worth the death penalty? And what about those innocent puppies that died? Certainly the Old Testament God would be on PETA's list of anti-animal deities. Did Yahweh destroy Sodom and Gomorrah because He hated homosexuals who gathered around Lot's house because they wanted to rape His beautiful angels?

Can there be something more than the literalness of these stories? If there isn't then the bible makes a good door stopper. I think there are more profound ways of understanding the Old Testament stories, at least most of them, than taking them literally.

For example, there are plenty of stories where God has made up His mind to slaughter everyone in a given town, or kill this or that family, or wipe out this or that tribe and then something changes His mind. Abraham got God to agree not to destroy Sodom and Gomorrah if he could find 10 good men (sadly, Abraham couldn't but it is also hard to find 10 good men in Washington D.C. so such a result shouldn't be surprising). And Moses was able to convince God not to kill *all* the Israelites when He found some of them partying up a pagan storm, dancing around the Golden Calf, probably naked and doing "it" all over the place, after giving Moses the commandments. Moses only wound up having to kill about 3,000 of them. Jonah walked through Nineveh telling everyone that God was going to destroy the city because of its sinfulness. Then God noticed that the people had actually transformed themselves into a good nation and God changed His mind.

Now, a literal translation shows God to be weak-willed in these cases. He spouts fire and brimstone (okay, He nailed Egypt and Sodom and Gomorrah) and then backs down. Seriously, is that the proper or best way to read these tales?

I think not.

Using God as a vehicle for explaining the world, we can look at such events and think, "The future is not set. Our decisions can change the course of events. We are not always fated by what we think of as fate." God changed His mind. If He can change His plans for the future, then that future is not written in stone.

Adam and Eve? The fruit they ate was the knowledge of good and evil, such knowledge you gain as you grow up. I think of my beautiful little grandchildren. They live in an innocent world right now. They don't know of death; they don't know of the immense sorrows the world might have in store for them. Soon they will go to school, meet those other kids (think of those little devils as serpents) and they will have left the Garden of Eden that their parents created for them. It will be the parents who send them out into the cruel world, much as God sent out Adam and Eve. Yes, in the story, God is punishing Adam and Eve for disobedience but that is the answer to where evil came from—after all, children first show their sense of self by wanting to do what they want to do which often means disobeying their parents—and such disobedience goes all the way through teenage years (think of all the movies highlighting wild drunken parties when the parents aren't home) to criminal or moral turpitude. Jealousy and murder become the first major sins of fallen mankind. The primitives who read this story now understood why they just had diarrhea.

In the context of growing up; in the context of gaining knowledge of the world in every way, shape and form, we all left the Garden of Eden long, long ago and got hammered by life. Is the tale one hundred percent perfect in its application to all of us? No. Some children are born outside the Garden of Eden right off. Even so, does the tale make far more sense now? It does to me.

That Adam-Eve story has some applicable resonance in my interpretation. Otherwise, God punished the entire human race with evil and death because two naked innocents ate a damn fruit! (Probably a fig since they were standing under a fig tree and put fig leaves on themselves when they realized they were naked.)

Anyway, as I look over the Old Testament, I still do not see proof of the existence of God in it, but I do see it as a lot finer book than I thought it was in the past. (Should I say "book" when talking about the Old Testament? It was written by many hands over many hundreds of years. It contains poetry, prose and song—and a great sexual story in "The Song of Solomon.")

Now the New Testament is something different. The angry and avenging Yahweh is transformed into a loving father, albeit one who allows His son Jesus to be crucified; kind of like all those fathers that have sent their sons off to war.

Paul was the first to write about Jesus and Jesus' meaning to us all. Paul was (to be kind) a little eccentric, postulating that the end of the world was really so close that husbands and wives should refrain from doing you-know-what so they could be pure. Paul wanted all married couples to be like those couples in the 1950s sitcoms who slept in separate beds or those aristocrats who slept in separate rooms.

Paul was a true theologian and he created a world plan that Jesus and you and I fit into. He was a visionary as well and an astute public relations man. He could see how the life of Jesus Christ could be wrapped and packaged to convert the whole world.

Paul was also the one who opened to the pagans the same right to follow Jesus as the Jews had. In fact, if it weren't for Paul, Christianity would have stayed a Jewish sect and would not have exploded as a world-wide religion. Paul did away with many of the Jewish customs, such as circumcision and the kosher laws (thank you Paul for now we can eat bacon!), so the pagans could continue their own basic customs which made it a lot easier for them to be converted. *("Iguanids, you do not have to cut part of your penis off to go to heaven." "Good, then I'll convert.")* Paul helped to make Christianity highly adaptable to the world at large.

But it isn't Paul who is the essence of Christianity; it is Jesus Christ. Yes, much of what Christ is reputed to have said are quotes from the Old Testament given vibrancy because of his charismatic personality. Yes, scholars have shown us that much of the four Gospels were written (or copied) by those who never knew or met Jesus (kind of ancient world PR men selling a product) and yes, many liberties were taken with the stories and events.

So what?

Those four Gospels (Matthew, Mark, Luke and John) are powerful; passed down for two thousand years, and still vibrating with truth. The words and parables of Jesus Christ in the Gospels and the words and works of William Shakespeare are the greatest of human expressions.

Now did Christ rise from the dead? How about all of the people who rose from the dead when Christ died? (Oh, yes, go back and read Matthew 50-54 and you'll see the rising from the dead of all those "others" when Christ passed. You don't hear much of that in church I'd dare say.) Is Christ one of the three "persons," along with The Father and The Holy Spirit, in a single God, known as the Trinity in Catholicism? Did he walk on water; raise other dead people such as Jarius' daughter and the more famous Lazarus? Could he feed a multitude with only a few fishes and some loaves of bread? Could he calm the storm; cure the blind and the lepers?

C.S. Lewis has an interesting argument for supporting all these stories about the miraculous Jesus. If Jesus didn't do these things, then he was just a madman who thought he was the savior of the world. So he must have done these things or we have postulated Godhood for a nut. (By the way, Jews should love Jesus because the whole Christian world, with very few exceptions, worships Jesus as God. You've got to love the irony—my Jewish friends love the fact that a Jew is the God of the Christians.)

I don't necessarily buy that argument of C.S. Lewis. Hamlet didn't exist, yet Hamlet is the most compelling character ever written by Shakespeare. Hamlet's words ring in your ears long after you have seen or read the play. Hamlet needn't exist for him to be a true expression of humanity. I think the same holds true for Jesus.

But that doesn't address the original question. Does *God* exist?

Okay, to close this, let me throw in a little mysticism. During the Mass, the priest does a ritual that Catholics believe creates the real body and blood of Jesus Christ that we then share. When I receive Communion I feel that I am spanning the centuries and partaking in the life of an extraordinary man. It does feel real to me even if Jesus never existed or never was a divine entity but was just a man.

Does God exist?

I don't know.

And, really, I don't care.

25

The Zombie Apocalypse

Bless me father for I have sinned.
I believe zombies hold the universal truth.

People wonder why so many of us love the zombie genre in both movies and literature. Zombies have been popular since George A. Romero's first flick *Night of the Living Dead* made its debut in 1968.

In that movie the zombies were actually called ghouls because ghouls are cannibals. However from that point on in picture after picture and book after book these ghouls became the modern-day zombies and the rest is history—bloody, intestine-spilling, goo-splattering history. Now there are even television shows highlighting the zombie apocalypse—which is the end of the world caused by the undead.

The basic outlines of the zombie story are well established. Suddenly, sometimes over a single night, dead people rise and start chewing on living people. Mom and Dad are sleeping peacefully in bed after a night of joyous coitus, the world is in its place and everything is just fine. Then their daughter, cute little Lulu with blood dripping on her face and seeping into her Doctor Denton's pajamas, creeps into the room, leaps on Dad and rips his throat out. Mom awakens and cute little Lulu takes a chunk out of her too.

Mom and Dad shortly thereafter die and turn into zombies. These two new zombies, and their adorable blood-spattered daughter, go after more living people for food. Some people will die completely after a zombie attack because the zombies have basically devoured everything mortal of that person including its brain. The only way to permanently kill a zombie is to shoot it in the head, stick a sharp object through its eyes into its brain, or blow its head off with a shotgun or grenade and the like. Shooting or stabbing a zombie in the chest can't kill it; it just gets blood and goo all over everybody near in the splatter zone.

What if a person is bitten buts gets away? Sadly, that person will ultimately die and also become a zombie. These new zombies will be ravenous (actually all zombies at all times are ravenous) and they will hunt living humans—and so it goes until the whole world is populated by these ravenous undead creatures and increasingly fewer living people can be found. Those living people who remain do everything they can to escape what is—probably—inevitable, their own deaths and the end of humanity as a species.

Scene after disgusting blood-soaked scene in movies, page after disgusting blood-soaked page in books, the zombies move forward trying to devour us. And they do. Most of the time the living people lose. That's why we often call it the "zombie apocalypse." It's the end of the world, the total end of everything we hold dear—starting with our own lives. Our military, our science, our medical community—none of our advanced knowledge can stop the undead from killing the rest of us. We have nuclear weapons; the zombies just have teeth and hunger. The zombies win.

The zombie apocalypse is all consuming. It happens everywhere. No culture, no country, no city, no town, no country farm community is spared the horror. Those creeping, crawling, staggering, bleeding, decomposing zombies must win—it is almost inevitable.

And that is—I am afraid—why the zombie genre is so loved and so important to aficionados. It holds the true meaning of life, totally unadorned by distracting bologna such as love and permanence and infinity; it is full of blood and guts and reality sans all sentimentality. Think; think carefully, each of us lives in our own zombie apocalypse. Death stalks us. It stalks us every day of our lives. Death is stalking you even as you read this. Death stalks everyone we love, everyone we hate, everyone everywhere around the world. There is no escape from it. Death is a single-minded monster geared to just one thing—the end of you, the end of your loved ones; *the* end of every person who ever took a breath.

Go to a hospital. Go to a doctor. Take your medicine. Do everything you can to be a healthier you—run, swim, lift weights, eat the right foods, limit your alcohol intake and guess what? Life will eat you and death will digest you. You cannot escape. Hide from death behind science; read the latest medical journals and guess what? Death still rules. And death is more often than not an ugly scene. Check out your local emergency room, the cancer ward or the operation rooms in the hospital and you will see that death is not pretty. It is as disgusting as a zombie movie. Death lives within the gore of illness, the monstrous slaughter in war. You cannot barricade yourself against death because it will break into your compound and take you. Zombies find ways to defeat all barricades used against them.

I have seen people I love die awful deaths, their bodies eaten away by disease; their brains masticated by Alzheimer's, their life forces shredded by such cruel fates. There is no escape. There is no place to run. There is no shelter. You can scream at God, "Why do *you* allow this?" but you will get no answer. God doesn't answer our pleas; He doesn't respond to our anger; He shows no sympathy for our agonizing sorrow and ultimate fate.

People you know can make all the excuses they want for the horror of it all ("Oh, there is a reason Frankie for all the pain and suffering and death. We just don't understand the reason. But God has a plan. And God is good.") but not one of the rationales makes sense or is comforting. The zombies are implacable. We know what they want. We need use no subtleties of reason explaining zombies. They eat us. They kill us. They win. Each man and woman's life is a horror by the end of it all.

The zombies win because they *must* win. Death is the strongest force on earth. You might think, "Well, even though we die our species lives on." No it doesn't. Nearly 90 percent of all species that have ever existed are now extinct—all their individuals are dead.

And now feast upon this—our entire planet will one day die. The zombie apocalypse is real—get used to it because that is the way it is, was and always will be.

26

Does God Exist?
Part Two

Bless me father for I have sinned. Death be not proud.

The last five years my father was crazy; certifiably crazy, hospitalized for awhile in a psychiatric unit crazy. This happened when my mother took ill with Alzheimer's and he refused to leave her side; he'd be with her all 24 hours and he tried to take care of her as best he could.

He refused to eat properly. ("When you are in your eighties, you don't have to eat.") He refused to drink liquids ("A couple of cups of decaf are all I need.") And he started his swift mental and physical decline. We even took him to the hospital to have them put an IV in him so he'd get hydrated. But we couldn't drive in every day from where we lived to force him to drink some water.

He barely slept.

Finally, he decided he couldn't change 12 diapers a night and he put my mom in a nursing home. He couldn't stand the thought that he did this, so he spun it, "You forced me to put her in a nursing home." If you knew my father you'd know I couldn't force him to do anything.

I took his car with the busted front window away from him. You could say I actually stole it from him. He was blind in one eye, had poor vision in the other eye, and the motor vehicle department had taken his license away. ("I don't need a license, I am a veteran.") On the road, he was a hazard. "I am very careful," he said on the day after he had slammed into the porch, denting the metal railing. By now my mother was dead and the house had to be sold so he'd have some money. My wife and I had supported my parents for several years but the time had come for him to get out of the house.

My lovely niece Melanie and I cleaned the house from top to bottom. There was dried feces everywhere. My mother had little control at the end and my father couldn't see what she was doing. I didn't want cleaners to come in and see this, so I spent several days on my hands and knees chipping away and scrubbing.

In the nursing home, two days before my mother died, Dad decided the two of them should take a walk. He lifted her semi-comatose body from the bed and she just slammed to the floor, as did he, and he was out cold. When he revived he denied he tried to get her to take a walk with him. The next day, the day before she died, he tried to get her to take another walk. They both went to the floor again. That day he told me she was looking better and they would be going on a cruise.

I said goodbye to my mother less than half a day before she died and my wife held her hand and gave mom permission to pass away. In fact, if you saw my mother, you would know that her soul or spirit had already left her weeks before. She was a dead person breathing.

After mom died, from the wake to her burial, my father was in a blind fury. He even made the funeral director cry with his verbal attacks. My wife and I had arranged for mom to be buried in a military cemetery where my father would join her when he died. They would be buried together.

Dad would have none of that. He wanted her buried in the plot where his mother was. I did as he desired, more to calm his fierce temper than for any other reason.

Nothing calmed him.

Day after day he would call me and scream about how horrible I was for taking his car away, for wanting to bury my mother in a grave that did not have his mother in it, about how veterans didn't have to follow the driving laws. He was convinced that thousands of people would want to visit my mother in the cemetery. He lashed out at my wife, calling her horrible names and telling her his real daughter-in-law was my ex-wife, who never liked him because she knew he had told me on the day I was to marry her, "Don't marry that girl; it won't work."

Finally, the house was sold and he moved into an apartment. He started wandering the streets trying to get hit by a car. It was then he went into the psychiatric hospital. After several months of care and five different medications, he was released and my niece arranged for him to go into a wonderful nursing home. And in three years, I visited him three times.

And he had been a terrific father.

When I was a young boy, he had taught me how to hit a baseball and how to play basketball. I excelled at those sports and got a full scholarship to a private high school. He came to every game that I played. He treated my friends and me to Yankee baseball games and pizza parties. He was funny; he was kind, and though he had a temper he would always say, "Frankie, I love you." Every day that I lived in my parents' home both of them at some point in that day would say, "Frankie, I love you."

He worked hard. He helped dozens of people with good counsel and money. He gave away money as if there were no tomorrow. His generosity was well known and many people took advantage of him. When his parents got old, he supported them. He made money and spent money.

I was in awe of him. I loved him.

I got the call from the nursing home on Sunday. "Your father has pneumonia. We are giving him antibiotics. He has other infections."

I knew the code. He was near death.

The Beautiful A.P. and I arrived at the nursing home on Tuesday morning. I was the health-care proxy. I saw him in his bed; a shriveled, wrinkled, ancient 88 year-old man with no teeth, breathing laboriously. He had Alzheimer's by now and his fingers were constantly fiddling with the sheets. He couldn't talk. One eye was dead; the other could still see somewhat. He went in and out of consciousness. The staff of the nursing home tried to give me encouragement, "He might spring back." And I thought, Spring back to what? I had visited three weeks before and he was slumped in the wheelchair, mostly oblivious to the world around him.

This was the man whose anger could shake the world and I thought at that moment, "Behold the man."

We had a private nursing group taking care of him and I told his nurse, "I don't want him taken to a hospital; I don't want any invasive procedures; no feeding tubes, none of that. I want him to have as much morphine as he needs; even if it is a very large dose. I do not want him to experience any pain at all." I was telling her, in code, that I wanted Dad to die, peacefully in his sleep.

Then my wife and I sat by his bedside and talked to him. A.P. told him everyone in the family was fine. They had jobs; the kids were doing well in school; marriages had taken place. Everything was fine. He didn't have to worry about anyone.

I told him that he had done a wonderful job as a father and grandfather and great grandfather. A.P. and I told him how much we loved him.

Once he turned and seemingly woke up and turned his head to look directly at me.

"Do you know who I am?" I asked. "You don't have to talk; just blink." He didn't blink but went back to fiddling with the sheet that covered him. He was far, far away.

The nurse told me that he had been seeing people, perhaps hallucinating. I know that some dying people see dead relatives and friends. Whether these are real events or just hallucinations was irrelevant to me; they signaled that the dying person was being called to pass away.

"Are you seeing your mother and father?" I asked. "How about mommy? What about Dorothy? And Frank, your brother? And what about Annie and Rocco and Mary and Tess and Phil and Robert and all your friends? Do you see them?" I listed as many people as I could remember. When I finished A.P. listed them once again. At times he seemed to respond to some of the names.

It was time to go. A.P. kissed him and moved away. I then moved closer. His good eye opened; he reached out his arm directly at me and I took his hand. He squeezed my hand—an extremely strong squeeze—and even lifted his head towards me. He was, at that moment, fully conscious and he whispered, "Frankie, I love you."

His head went back onto the pillow; he closed his eyes, his fingers fiddled with the sheets and he died several hours later.

I wrote this on Christmas. I am 65 years old. I miss my parents.

27

The Humor of God

Bless me father for I have sinned. I doubt God's sense of humor.

Are we really made in the image and likeness of God? Does that mean we are physically like God or spiritually like God? Okay, to be clear, let's just say we have certain traits which are similar to God's and leave it at that.

But we certainly have a trait that God doesn't seem to have—a sense of humor—and that might make us somewhat superior to this divine being, at least in that one category. That's right, no matter where you find mankind, you find he has a sense of humor that allows him to laugh. He tells jokes; he performs pranks—sometimes his humor is nasty, sometimes gross, sometimes it is attempted but fails. Nevertheless, we are one fun-loving species Mankind when all is said and done is an undeniable laugh riot.

Not so God. Never God. Not once for God. No laughs there. No comedy club for Him.

Read the whole Old Testament and you won't see Yahweh busting a gut at something or playing a funny prank on someone. Why is that? Christians don't have it any better either. The New Testament is really dry. Not only is God still without humor; His son, our Lord Jesus Christ, the Second Person of the Blessed Trinity is also totally without a funny bone. Unless the Holy Spirit is a laugh riot, the Catholic God and (I assume) all the versions of the biblical God are sans humor as well. At least there are no laughs in the "good book" that have come down to us. I mean is this possible? Not a shred of humor in a book that is a few thousand pages?

Now, some quick-witted readers might say, "God is funny because he created man, yuck, yuck, yuck." Sorry, God is not portrayed as hooting and hollering by creating such flawed beings as Adam and Eve. If you think it funny that God created us, that is *our* humor coming into play by transferring it to Our Lord; it certainly is not God's humor. After all, God didn't have Adam and Eve *slip* on the fruit of the Knowledge of Good and Evil thereby landing on their asses in a hilarious moment immortalized in the book of Genesis. Instead, He sentenced them (and us) to death. No laughs there that I can see.

If God were an actor, He'd be deadpan. He'd be the lead in one of those shows that is constantly killing off major characters.

All the major and minor stories in the entire bible show God not to have a lick of a funny bone in Him. And that's sad, too, because so many stories could have used some humorous, or sarcastic, or slapstick or lighter elements to make them more riveting.

Do not fear. I have come to save the reputation of our Lord, the creator of the universe, the Supreme Being—I have discovered that He does have a sense of humor!

I shall now blow the lid off something no one knows—except me and soon you.

As I said above, God did have a sense of humor in the bible; yes, He did. However, over the millenniums, pious Jewish scribes and cloistered medieval Catholic monks erased all evidence of His sense of humor. They erased all evidence of humor in biblical characters too. They were convinced that God should be a dour father who only gave punishments, not grins, and they then went about fixing the divine being to make Him more like them. I mean, have any of you read any scribe or monk humor? Talk about dour! So in reality these writers of the "word" screwed up big time by trying to create God in their own pious images and likenesses and they succeeded in hijacking the "word"—and that's no joke. They also erased all evidence that great biblical characters such as Adam, Eve, Cain, Abel, Jacob, Solomon, Moses, David, Jesus and Paul had a great wealth of humor that they displayed all the time. Some of this humor has come down to us this very day as you shall see, even though we never knew it started in the bible.

Let me give you some examples gleaned from my extensive research involving the sense of humor found in the original and real bible.

The smartest man whoever lived was supposedly Solomon. Solomon had a peculiar habit—he always wanted to marry various princesses from all the tribes he could find. Some writers think good ole Solomon had some 700 wives, not to mention another 300 concubines. Whew! Talk about the Playboy channel! He died at 80 too—kind of like Hugh Hefner who died many years ago and is now a zombie.

But one day a wrung-out Solomon stood on the doorstep of the Temple and said to all his fellow Israelites, "Take my wives . . . please!"

One early morning when one of his Temple guards approached the hung-over Solomon who was recovering after a night of heavy drinking and unmentionable carnal acts, the guard said, "Sire, two women are here each claiming to be the mother of the same baby. What should we do?"

"My head is splitting in two," said Solomon.

"Yes, sire, I shall follow your command," said the guard.

Moses had a wonderful sense of humor. He had God send a great plague of frogs, one of which stuck in the Pharaoh's throat, causing the Pharaoh to talk as if, well, as if he had a frog in his throat. His voice became so squeaky with that frog blocking his voice box that this is how he sounded: "I shall not (squeak, squeak) let the Israel—(squeak)—ites go (squeak, squeak) because (squeak, squeak, squeak) . . . for Osiris's sake (squeak) will one (squeak) of (squeak) my magicians (squeak, squeak, squeak) get this (squeak) damn (squeak) thing out of (squeak, squeak) my throat?" There were snickers of laughter from Moses and Aaron and the other Hebrews at this meeting although Moses was heard to say, "You can't always get what you want but if you try sometime, you just might find you get what you need." Sadly the Hebrews did not get what they wanted—freedom—but they did get a few good laughs.

It wasn't a rain of locusts but a downpour of banana peels that caused all the Egyptians to go slipping and sliding on their cobblestone streets. Those Egyptians working atop the pyramids just went skidding down the slick sides to the sands below to the great amusement of the Israelites who were busy making bricks and laughing their heads off.

In addition, Moses did not call forth the Angel of Death to kill all the first born males of Egypt for that would be too cruel; instead he sent the angel of gastrointestinal flatulence which caused the entire empire to be enveloped in a hideously smelling methane cloud. This became known as the "pillar of cloud" in the bible once those scribes and monks ruined the original story; and when the Egyptians discovered they could burn this gaseous mass it became known as the "pillar of fire."

Sadly these witty plagues got changed because the scribes and monks did not want anyone to know that Moses and God were playing the Pharaoh and Egyptians for fools. These writers of the "word" edited out the paragraph that mentioned the fact that the Pharaoh became the laughing stock of all royalty during the 14 century B.C. That was the greatest punishment he could have suffered—being an object of scorn across the whole of the known world.

Moses didn't just zip-zap the Pharaoh; he played a delightfully funny prank on the children of Israel too. He said unto them, "Follow me and walk this way!" He then did a silly walk which the Hebrews mimicked, a silly walk that lasted 40 years, having them scurry through the desert before he laughingly announced, "We have finally found the Chinese restaurant with the best carry out!" Even his brother Aaron, a well-known stick-in-the-mud, laughed at that one.

Noah couldn't escape God's riotous humor. God told Noah to put two of every kind of animal on the ark. Noah did this. Then God told Noah that he had to tell his wife that she was in charge of cleaning up all the monstrous piles of poop these animals were pouring out of their butts. Even back in those days, wives could be hard to handle and asking his wife to clean up millions of pounds of poop a day did not sit well with her. You will note that Noah started out the story with three sons and ended the story with three sons. In those days a woman had as many kids as she could—so why didn't Noah and his wife procreate some more? If you were Noah's wife would you give him the time of day, much less another child, with all that shit?

In fact, Noah's name is a great joke. His real name was Sidney. So why do we now call him Noah? Well, Sidney used to go to his wife when he wanted sex and say, "Hey, baby, let's do 'ah' tonight, okay?" But after cleaning out all that crap on the ship, his wife would shoot back," No 'ah' for you!" And thus he got his name, No-ah.

Switching over to the New Testament, we see the real story of Pontius Pilate is somewhat different than the story as presented in the scripture. Pilate was a man totally devoid of wit and humor; the Roman guards used to love playing jokes on him. They played jokes on him all the time—many of them cruel jokes too. So at the most serious moment in the Passion of Christ (that's the time when Jesus is brought before Pilate, then is whipped, then is crowned with thorns, then is crucified), Pilate takes out a bowl of what he thinks is water and washes his hands in it saying, "I wash my hands of this man."

When he said that line his Roman guards roared with laughter. Pilate turned to his servant and said, "This water is yellow. Were the pipes rusty?"

"No, your eminence," snickered the servant as the guards roared. "You mistakenly took the chamber pot."

The Apostle Paul was a comic card. He jokingly told all the followers of Jesus to give up sex if they could—even if they were married. He never meant this. He was kidding around. What the heck else was there to do in those long, lonely evenings before X-rated movies? No one was going to give up sex but wouldn't it be fun to play a joke on the new Christians by asking them to? He even called the recommendation the "No-Ah" in honor of Noah but the monks removed this when they recopied Paul's works.

Perhaps the one book of the New Testament that has been involved in more movies and learned treatises is the "Revelation of John" also known as "The Book of Revelation." Probably half the movies with the devil in it point out this book and many people think it is a serious scriptural text. It wasn't. It was a total goof.

Here is the conversation between John and his Thymus, known as Tim, which proves what the Revelation was really all about. It was found on a parchment in a cave next to the Dead Sea Scrolls' cave. Those scrolls were also believed by early Christians to be a satire on crazed men wanting to live alone in the desert in caves.

Tim: Just read that thing you wrote.
John: Did you enjoy it?
Tim: What the hell was it about?
John: Oh, man, come on Tim. It's an all-out farce.
Tim: I thought so!

John: I modeled the Whore of Babylon after that wench we met at the Romulus and Remus orgy we went to. The beast with 666 was that big fat dude that we called Gigantus Maximus Tiny Penicus. And what about those four horsemen of the apocalypse with two of them being mares? Woe! That will confuse people, right? I have angels and demons and monsters and things in the story that are so stupid a person would have to be sniffing the fumes at the Oracle at Delphi to believe anything in the book. Ha! Ha!

Tim: But why did you write this thing? We're all laughing at it in my family; we kinda knew you were screwing around but in the future people might think this is real. We'll look like idiots to them.

John: Tim, Tim, Tim, we Christians need to lighten up. The people in the future can't be stupider than the people today. Just about everyone who has read this has gotten a good laugh out of it or at least a little chuckle. We're being persecuted all over the world. We need to have a little fun with what we're reading. You know I heard Paul is jokingly telling everyone not to have sex! And he's a Roman too! Have you ever known a Roman to turn down a boffing?

Tim: Do people believe him?

John: Some of the pious ones. How stupid can they be? Why would anyone recommend giving up one of life's pleasures? Most of the Christians are getting good laughs out of it. You know, Paul is a hoot. That thing he does when he falls to the floor twitching and drooling and saying he sees "the light" is a riot!

Yes, there are more examples of the witty humor in the bible but these few should suffice. I am happy that I found such lost humor because otherwise one would be seriously disappointed that a book that was to tell you all you needed to know about life, death, God and all He created, lacked a single laugh.

28

What Did Jesus Believe?

Bless me father for I have sinned. I don't think Jesus told us anything new.

Catholics, Protestants, Ultra-Christians, Evangelicals, Christian snake handlers, small cults surrounding some slick-haired or wild-eyed preachers, end of the world Christians, Jehovah's Witnesses, Anabaptists such as the Amish, Quakers, Christian soldiers ala Salvation Army . . . I am guessing the list of Christian sects and beliefs can go on and on.

The beliefs of various Christians run the gamut from believing Christ was God to believing he was a great prophet but not divine. He was part of a Trinity composed of God the Father; God the Son and God the Holy Spirit. Or there is no Trinity. Jesus had a wife; he didn't have a wife. He had children; he didn't have children. He was white; he was black or some other color in between. He was tall; he was short. He was gay; he was straight.

Theologically I really don't care what various Christians believe as long as they aren't shoving it in my face or, more important, trying to kill me because they think that is what God wants of his children—universal slaughter of the unbelievers.

In my opinion, the various Christian beliefs are irrelevant.

Wars have been fought over whether the Pope is the supreme power of Christendom or whether he is the anti-Christ and/or Satan himself. Mary was a virgin her entire life or she had a host of kids which meant she and Joseph did the deed. There's free will; there isn't free will. Drinking is wrong; drinking is okay. Cover your head ladies or don't cover your head ladies. Grow a beard; don't grow a beard.

I really don't care what you believe, so enough already. Don't ring my doorbell with *your* truth because I do not care to hear it.

You see, all of Christendom has missed the essential, fundamental point. It isn't what Catholics believe or what other Christians believe or what the doorbell ringers believe. It is what *Jesus* believed. It is what Jesus *knew*. That is the ultimate test. That is the ultimate answer to the question of who Christ was.

To make matters simple—all the religious beliefs of Christ about himself, about Judaism, about being the Messiah are also irrelevant if Christ's other beliefs are wrong! Christ just has to be wrong in one thing and he isn't God—he isn't some Divine Messiah—he isn't anyone at all except a preacher with a good line and a relatively loyal following.

Here's a list of some (just some) of the major questions I have about Christ's beliefs and the problems occurring with them.

Question: Did Christ believe in the *literal* interpretation of the Garden of Eden story in Genesis? Did he believe there existed a talking serpent? Did he believe in the Tree of the Knowledge of Good and Evil?

Problem: If he did believe this account to be literally true, he was content with the fact that all of mankind was punished with death for Adam and Eve's eating of a fruit. He also believed that the talking serpent was transformed into a snake. Or did he think the serpent was the devil as Catholics are taught? If he thought of the story merely as a metaphor why didn't he say this in his teachings? There is no hint that he rejected the literalness of the story. Would rejecting the literal interpretation make him part ways with Judaism since it was an accepted literal interpretation among his fellow Jews? Was the story real or not? Jesus, what did you believe?

Religious Beliefs: Some Christians believe the Garden of Eden story is literal and it took place a shade under 6,000 years ago. Most Catholics believe that the story is merely a metaphor to explain how evil entered the world. Which idea is true? Which did Jesus believe?

Question: Is the Cain and Abel story literally true? Was Cain thrown out of the Garden to wander the world but was concerned with being killed by all the people out there?

Problem: Where did all these people "out there" come from? Did Jesus believe the myths about Lilith being Adam's first "wife" and procreating with demons and animals to create the race of beings that Cain feared? Did he buy this idea? He never mentions it.

Religious Beliefs: Many reasons are given for the "other" people being out there—all the early offspring of Adam and Eve were born as fraternal twins, meaning one boy and one girl, or Lilith created them. Or the story is merely to show that jealousy leading to serious sins such as murder existed in our very first ancestors—even if those ancestors were not actually Cain and Abel. So where does Jesus throw his lot? The story is a cautionary tale that didn't happen as written or it is absolutely true as it was written? So which is it Jesus? Give us some idea of what you think.

Question: Did Jesus believe that the world was actually and entirely flooded because God was disappointed in what mankind had become? Did God kill off every land animal on earth but had Noah save a pair of each on an ark not big enough to fit the Bronx zoo? Or did Jesus know this story was a metaphor? Did he reject the literal interpretation? Is Noah actually the Father of all humanity since he and his family were the only ones saved? Jesus, was this story real or not?

Problem: Jesus never says how he views this story—is it real, totally imagined, or an exaggeration of an historical event? Since getting all those animals on such a small ship was impossible did God perform some miracle to do this? Tell us Jesus.

Religious Beliefs: Some Christians believe it is literally true and Noah with God's help figured out how to get all the animals on earth into the ark. Since the literalists do not reject the existence of dinosaurs (monsters) then these creatures had to make it onto the ark as well. Or is this just another story to explain catastrophes since the size of the ark was ridiculously small for such a gigantic undertaking? What did Jesus believe?

So Many More Questions: Was the Sodom and Gomorrah story literally true? Does God hate gays or just people who are unfriendly and prone to rape? Did Jacob literally wrestle with an angel or with God depending on the translation of the bible you read? Did God send 10 plagues and wipe out the first born Egyptians and cripple their entire society? Did God destroy the entire army of Pharaoh? Did God harden the Pharaoh's heart thereby making the Pharaoh a mere puppet in the story? Did God really intend to kill all the Israelites when they partied while Moses was on Mt. Sinai getting the commandments?

Problems: You are getting the picture I am drawing—what was Jesus' real belief system? Was he a literalist? Did he look at these tales merely as stories? Were the prophecies of the coming Messiah real or just fanciful stories to him? Was Mary really impregnated by God? Come on, Jesus, we have some real issues here.

Now let's go even deeper into what confuses me. Let's take a look at science or at least what we know with our current science. What does Jesus believe or know to be the truth?

Did he know about germs?

Did he know of and believe in the atomic theory of matter?

Did he believe in evolution?

Did he know about the theory of relativity?

How old did he think the earth was?

Did he know the earth is oval and not flat?

Did he know which suns and planets have life?

You see the conundrum? If Jesus believed the earth is flat then he obviously isn't God and he obviously is not any more advanced than the other people of his time and place. If he did know the earth is oval why didn't he tell people this? Why hide the truth?

If he knew about germs why not help us create penicillin instead of just healing this or that individual person? Penicillin might be a greater miracle than curing some single leper.

In short, what was Jesus' belief system? What did he really know about things? Certainly he knew about morality—but is Hell real? Is it just a burning pit outside Jerusalem? Is it just a metaphor? Which way of looking at this is the way to look at this? All the interpretations can't be right. Hell either exists or it doesn't exist. Germs exist or they don't exist.

Did Jesus know about nuclear weapons? How the atoms could be smashed to make an explosion even greater than the one that leveled Sodom and Gomorrah?

On and on and on and on it goes.

What did Jesus know? *What did he know?*

Why didn't he just level with us? If he understood the world as we now do why not just come out and say it? Sure doing such a thing would confound the people of his day but so what? He was confounding most of them already. Wasn't he a teacher? So teach us something we never heard about before. It certainly would make the literalist beliefs wrong. So what? That would certainly show that he was more than just some moralist wandering around a small area telling people this is good and that is bad. If he were God incarnate why not give us something that only God would know— some secret that would explode all the things that were wrong with the bible or that would be wrong in the future.

For example, "Do not believe in the theory of evolution. No creature can change into some other creature and here is absolute proof of what I am saying." Or, "Evolution is real and the story of the creation of earth six thousand years ago is just a fable. It never happened and here is absolute proof of what I am saying." Or, "The earth is not the center of the universe. It revolves around the sun. Here is proof." Or, "Those people who believe the earth is at the center of the universe and the sun revolves around it are correct and here is proof of what I am saying."

My dilemma is not what I believe or what you believe or what he or she believes. I really don't care what you believe. Your beliefs are meaningless. I do not see a way out of my dilemma. I wish I did. Faith cannot answer my questions. "Have faith, Frankie, Jesus knew the truth about it all." Really, so where is that truth? I agree with Pilate when he asked Jesus, "And what is truth?" even though I recognize Pilate was being sarcastic. Is truth in Adam? Eve? Noah? Moses? Einstein? Darwin? Is it in a virus, a bacterium, out among the stars? Jesus, what did you believe? You are silent on the most important stuff. A simple statement that no one of your time would be able to make would be more than sufficient to seal the deal.

My dilemma is the dilemma of what did Jesus believe; what did Jesus know? If I knew that I would truly know him and that is—simply—what I want. If he was just a preacher, fine. He has a lot to say that is strong and good. If he really knew that those stories in the bible were just tales, fine, he was quite advanced. If he knew everything—even things we have just discovered such as the Higgs Boson—great, great, that's great.

You know something? Jesus didn't even have to shout these "truths" from the mountain tops. He could have just turned to Peter or any other disciple and said, "Oh, by the way my son, write this down and don't bother publicizing it but someday people will know what I am talking about. Quantum mechanics is right and as Einstein discovered the universe is made of mass and energy that are interchangeable and this mass and energy is in everything—living and non-living things. Things pop in and out of existence and an apple will fall on your head because of gravity. And Galapagos Island will turn the world of life on its head for real. Just mark my words."

I would be totally satisfied with that because right now we don't really know what Jesus knew and believed. And there is the crux.

Still and all, training and upbringing, habit and comfort, I am a Catholic through and through and, even if I *am* a little wayward . . . it's been fun being Catholic. (Although after these last few chapters I am once again afraid of being hit by THE BUS.)

MAY X 2014

8/16

Made in the USA
Lexington, KY
16 March 2014